KEVIN GARNETT

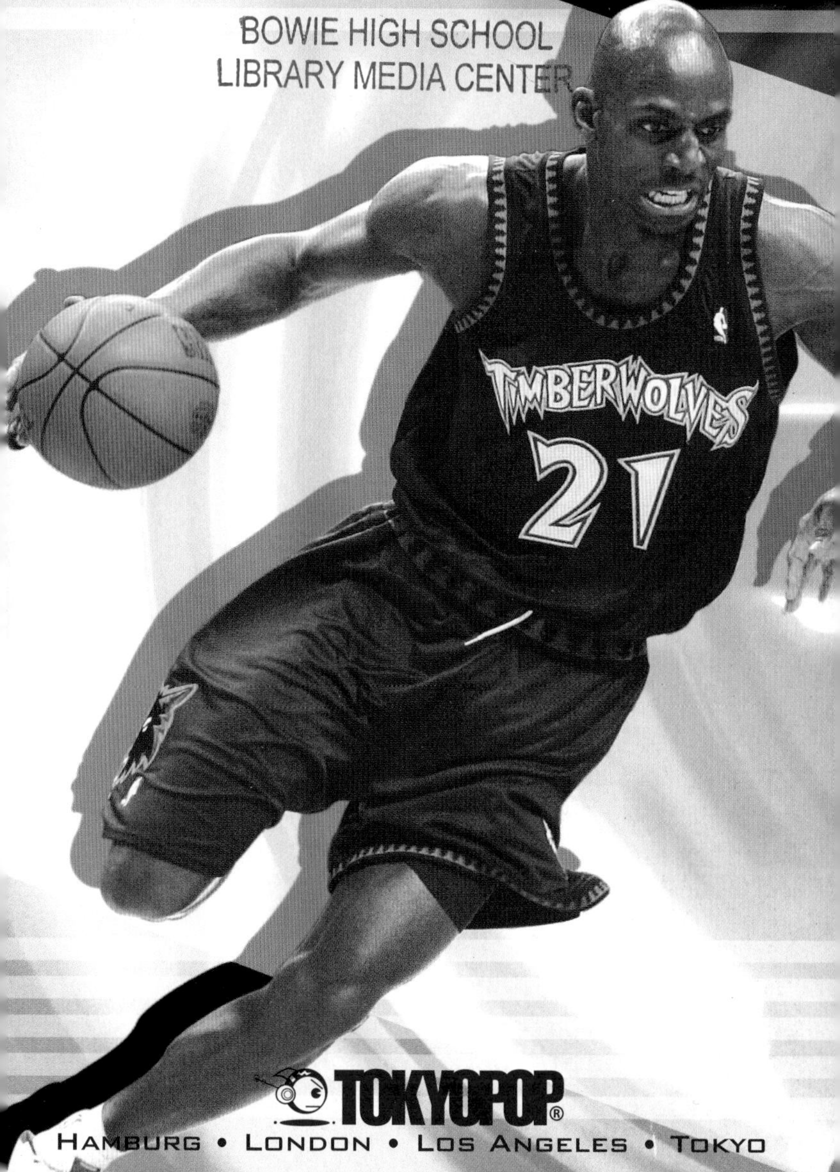
TIMBERWOLVES
21

TOKYOPOP®

HAMBURG • LONDON • LOS ANGELES • TOKYO

Graphic Design and Lettering - Jennifer Nunn-Iwai,
& Tomás Montalvo-Lagos
Cover Layout - Matt Alford
Character Design - Tomás Montalvo-Lagos
Illustrations - Michael Paolilli and Tomás Montalvo-Lagos

Editor - Jod Kaftan
Digital Imaging Manager - Chris Buford
Pre-Press Manager - Antonio DePietro
Production Managers - Jennifer Miller and Mutsumi Miyazaki
Art Director - Matt Alford
Senior Editor - Elizabeth Hurchalla
Managing Editor - Jill Freshney
VP of Production - Ron Klamert
Editor-in-Chief - Mike Kiley
President & C.O.O. - John Parker
Publisher & C.E.O. - Stuart Levy

E-mail: info@TOKYOPOP.com
Come visit us online at www.TOKYOPOP.com

A TOKYOPOP® Cine-Manga® book

TOKYOPOP Inc.
5900 Wilshire Blvd., Suite 2000
Los Angeles, CA 90036

GREATEST STARS OF THE NBA: KEVIN GARNETT

ISBN: 159532-184-5
First TOKYOPOP® printing: February 2005

10 9 8 7 6 5 4 3 2 1

Printed in China

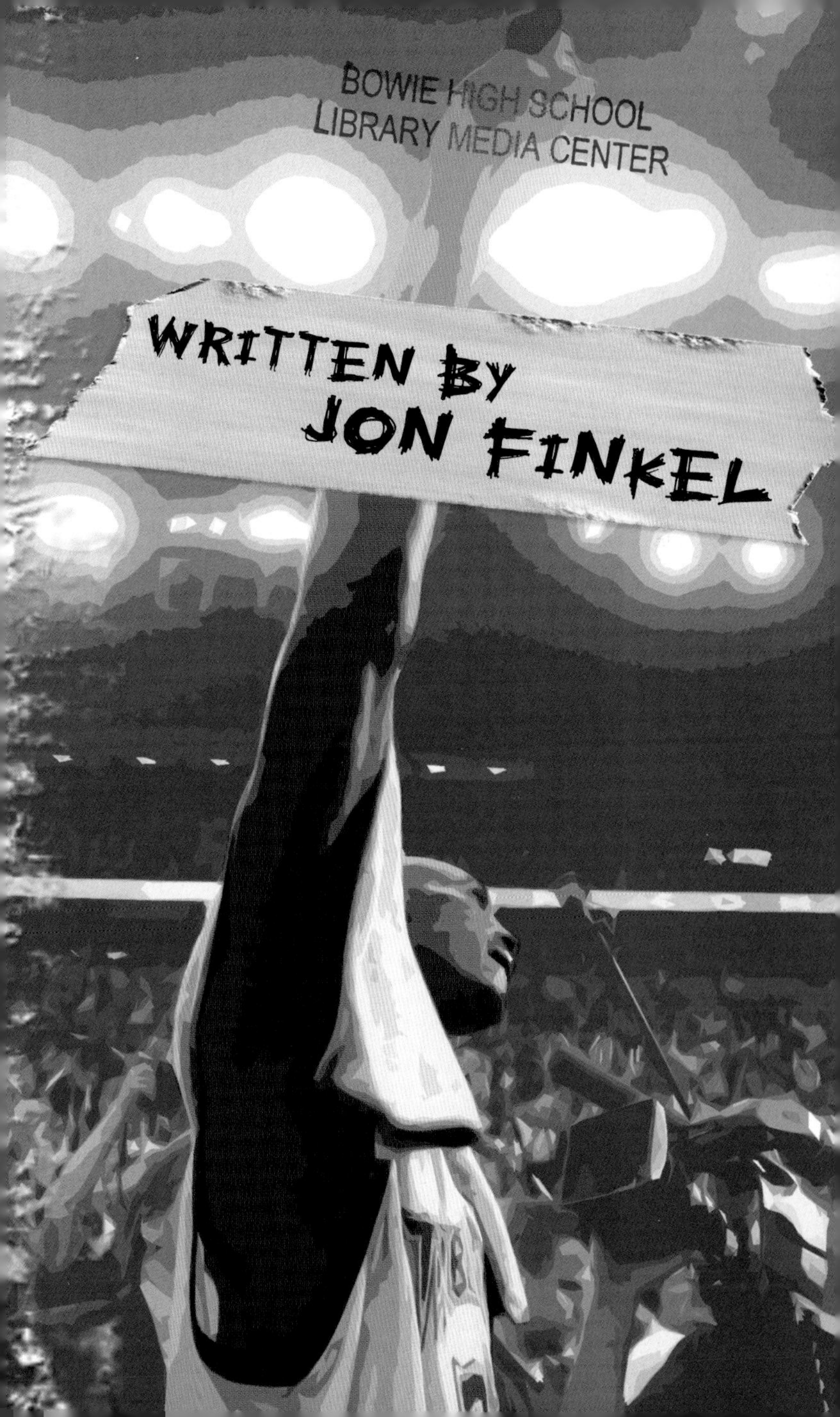

BOWIE HIGH SCHOOL
LIBRARY MEDIA CENTER
WRITTEN BY
JON FINKEL

CONTENTS//:

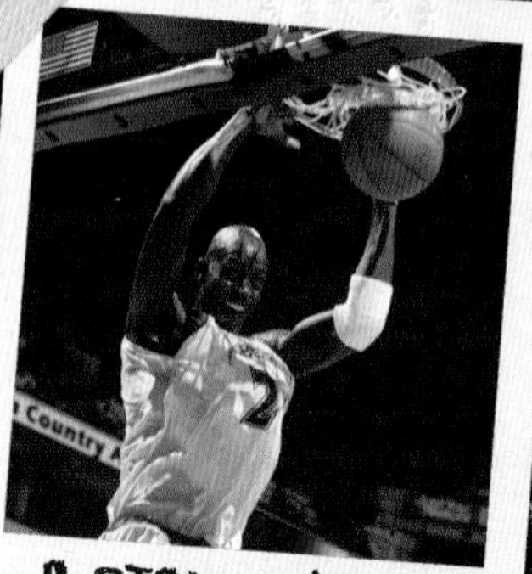

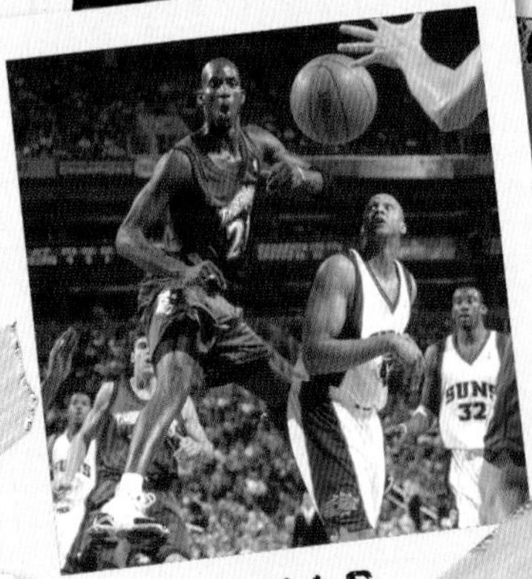
SUNS
32

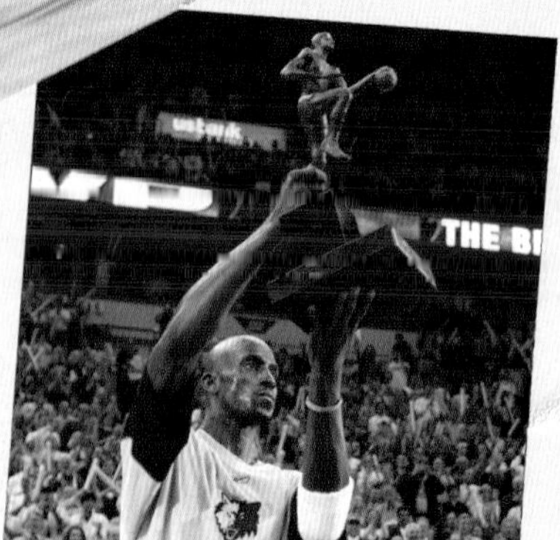

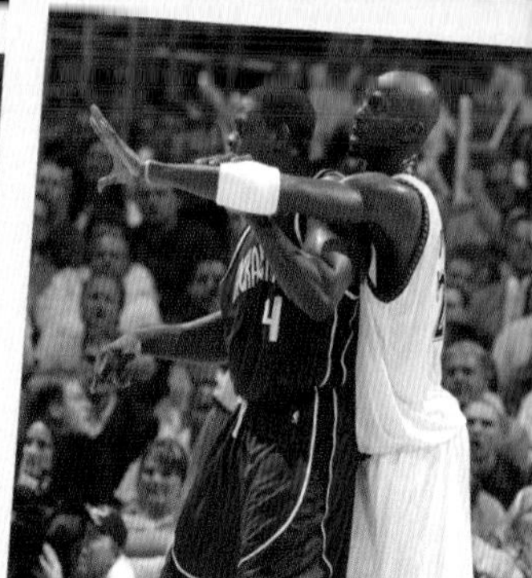

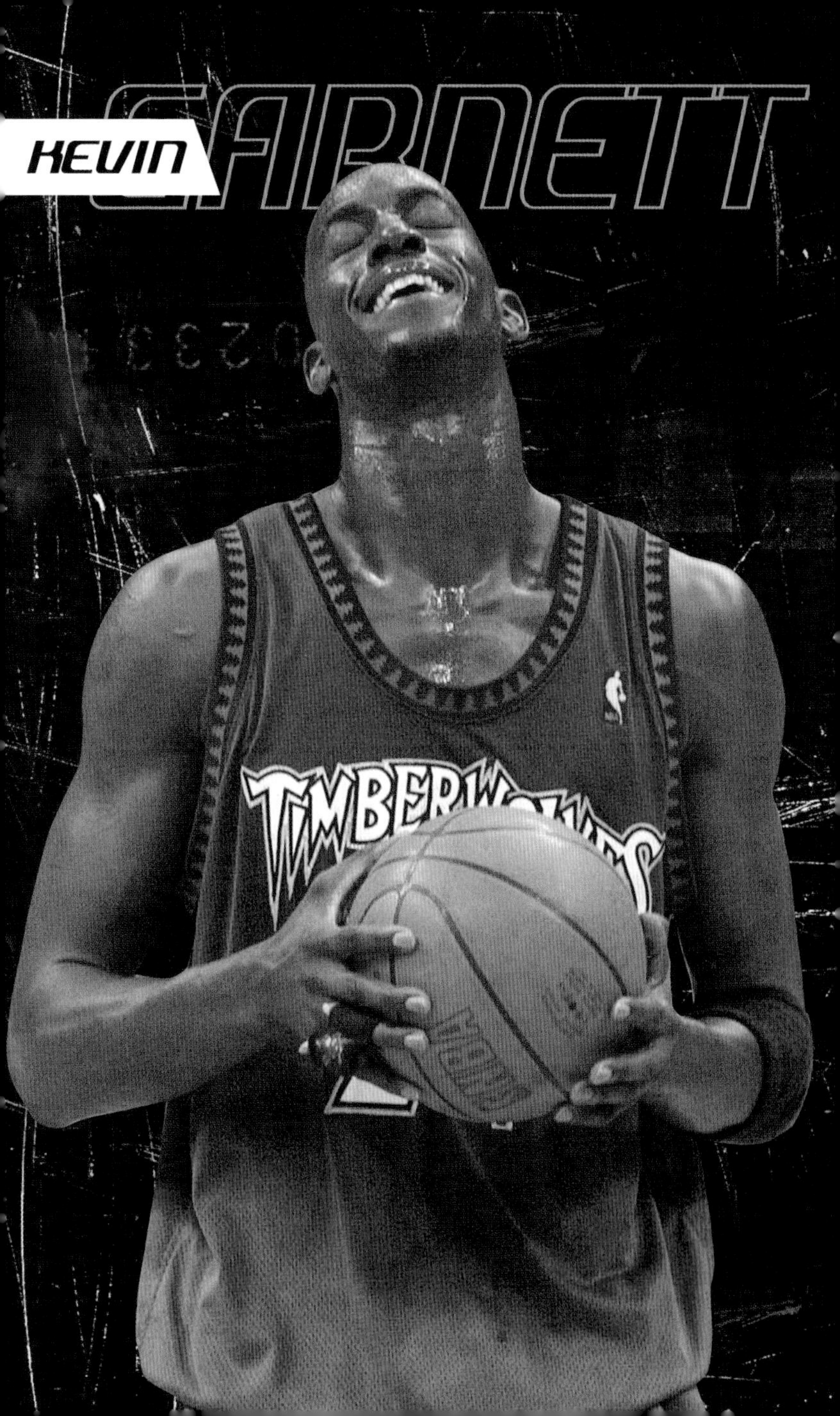
KEVIN
GARNETT

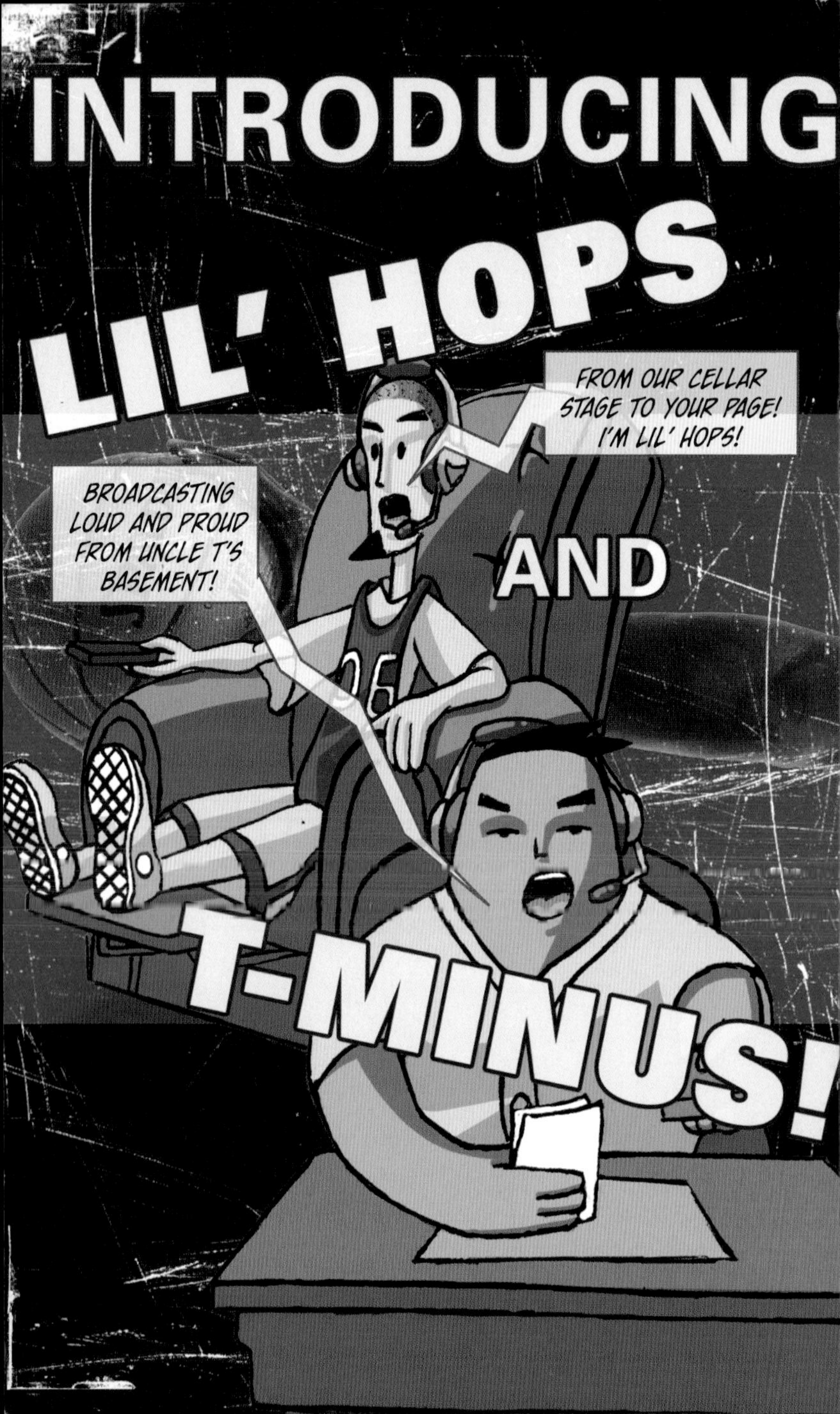
INTRODUCING
LIL' HOPS
FROM OUR CELLAR STAGE TO YOUR PAGE! I'M LIL' HOPS!
BROADCASTING LOUD AND PROUD FROM UNCLE T'S BASEMENT!
AND
T-MINUS!

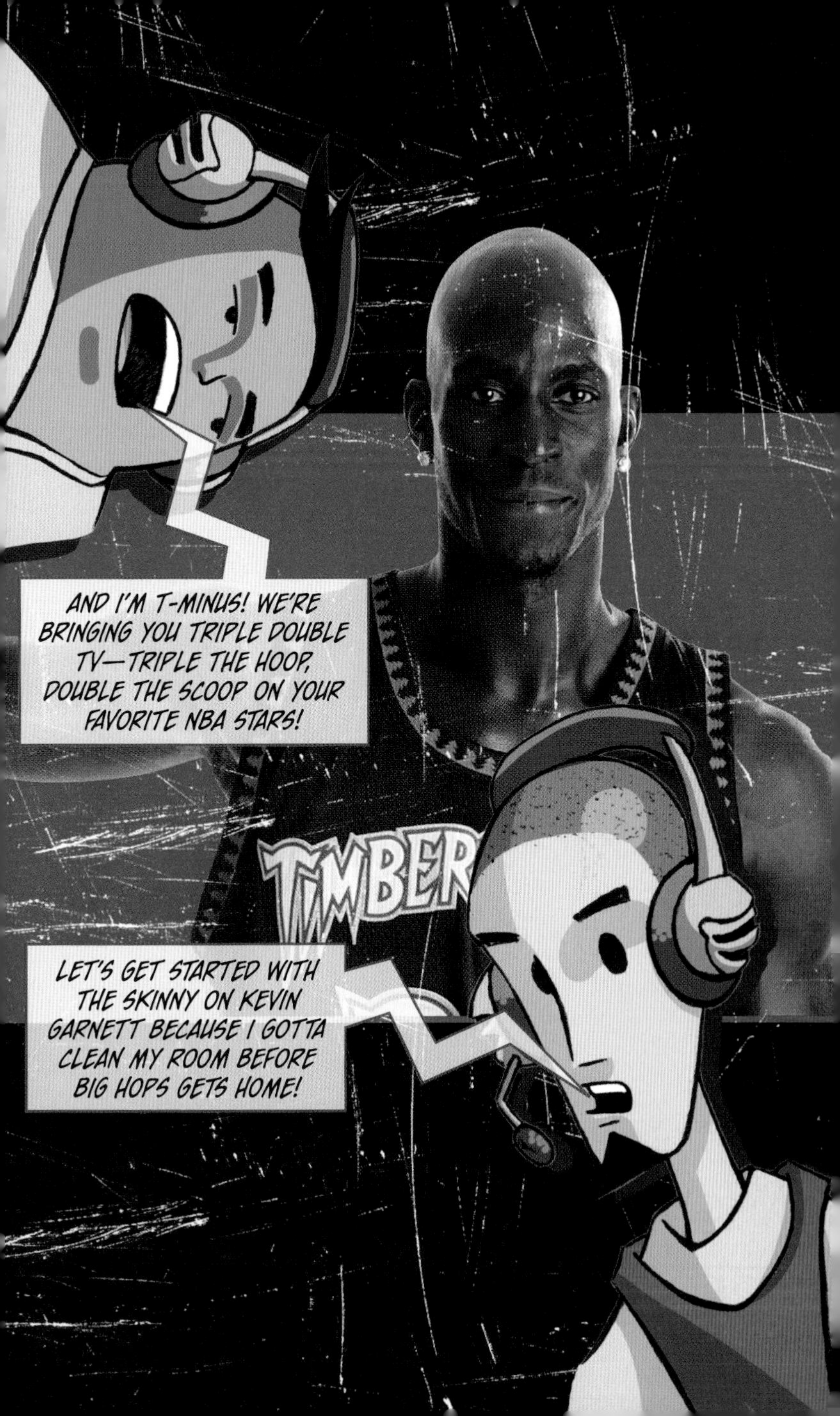
AND I'M T-MINUS! WE'RE BRINGING YOU TRIPLE DOUBLE TV—TRIPLE THE HOOP, DOUBLE THE SCOOP ON YOUR FAVORITE NBA STARS!
LET'S GET STARTED WITH THE SKINNY ON KEVIN GARNETT BECAUSE I GOTTA CLEAN MY ROOM BEFORE BIG HOPS GETS HOME!
TIMBER

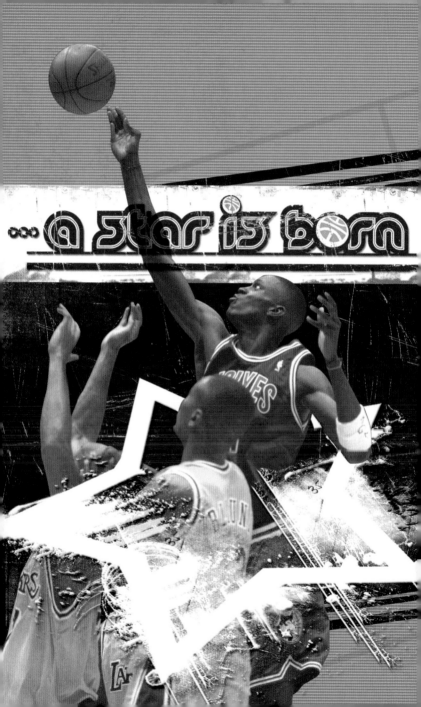

...a star is born

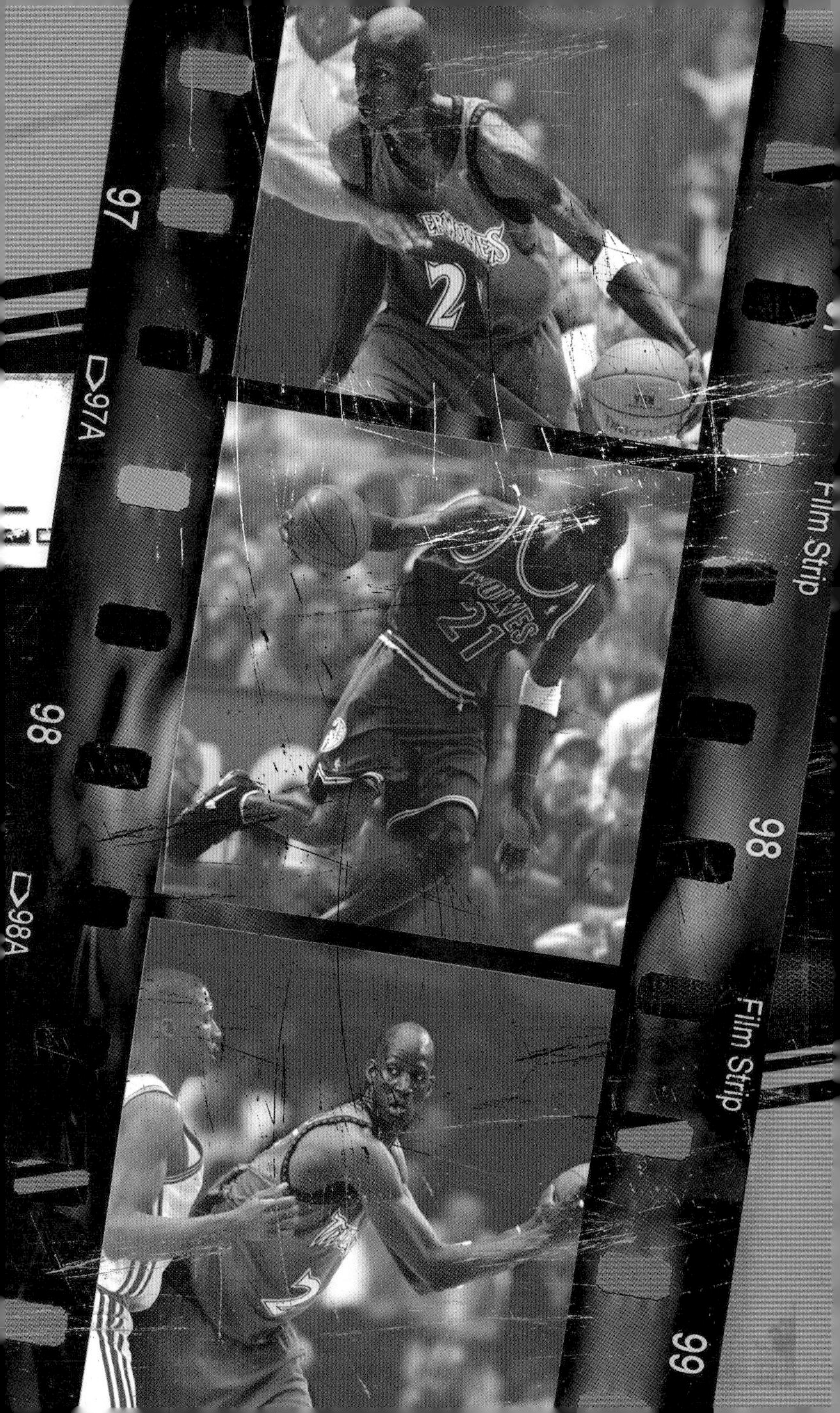

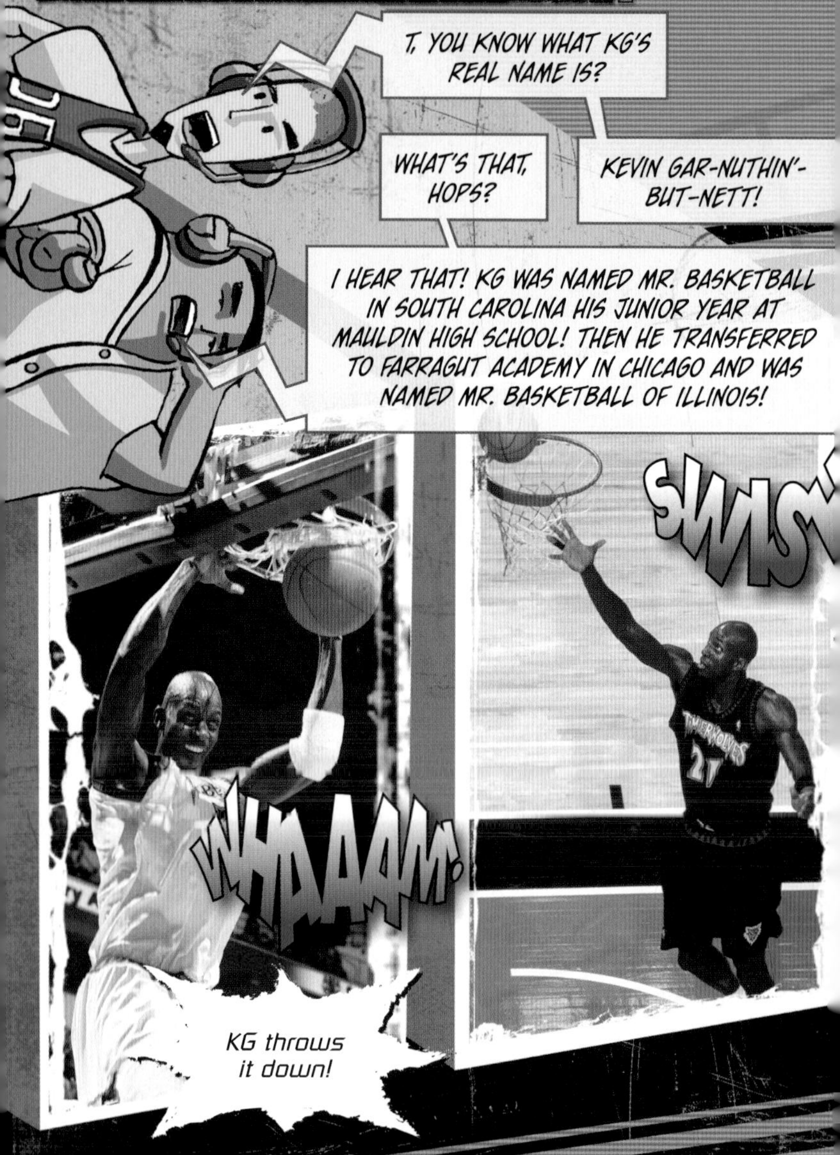
T, YOU KNOW WHAT KG'S REAL NAME IS?
WHAT'S THAT, HOPS?
KEVIN GAR-NUTHIN'-BUT-NETT!
I HEAR THAT! KG WAS NAMED MR. BASKETBALL IN SOUTH CAROLINA HIS JUNIOR YEAR AT MAULDIN HIGH SCHOOL! THEN HE TRANSFERRED TO FARRAGUT ACADEMY IN CHICAGO AND WAS NAMED MR. BASKETBALL OF ILLINOIS!
WHAAAM!
KG throws it down!

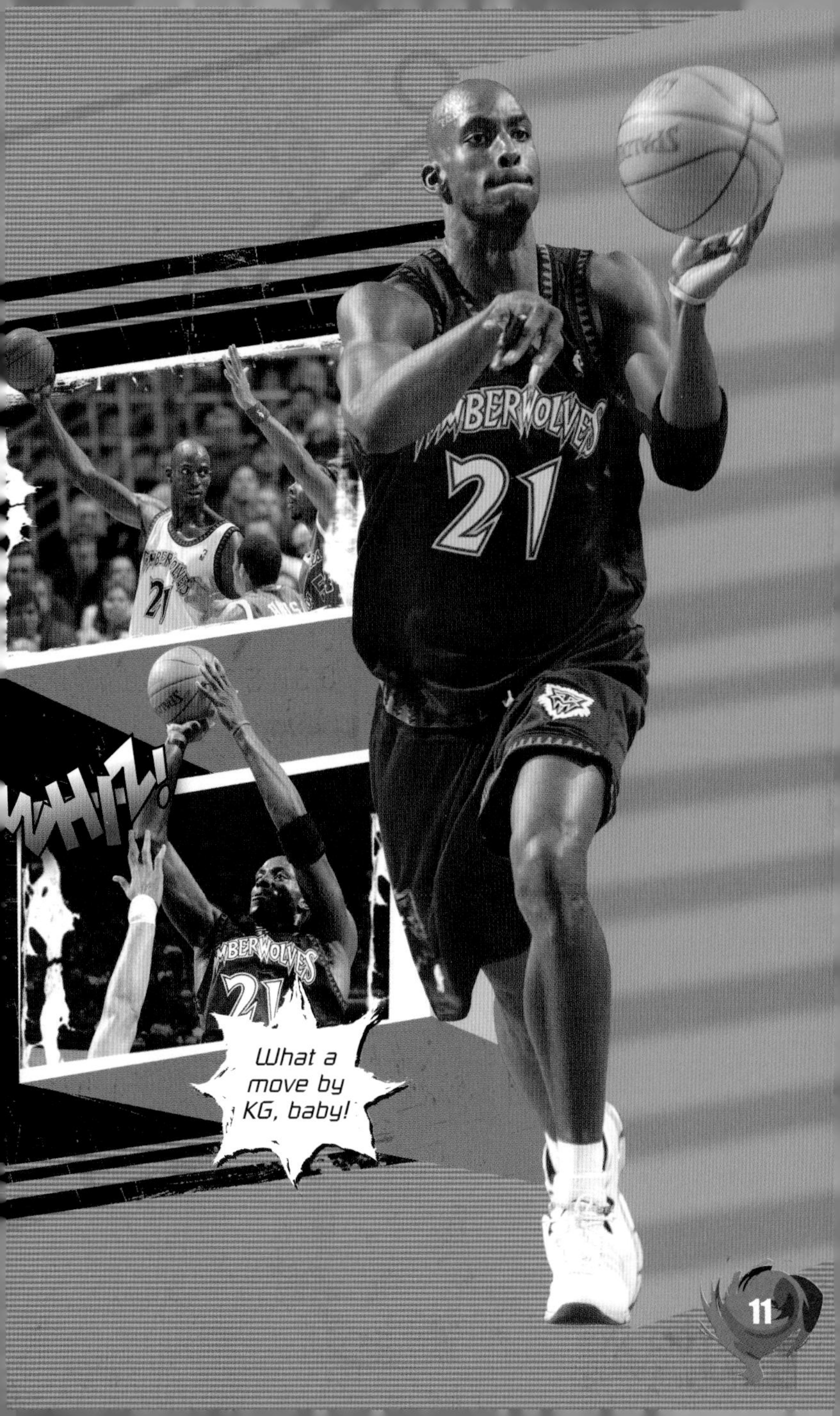
TIMBERWOLVES
21
WHIZ!
What a
move by
KG, baby!

...a star is born

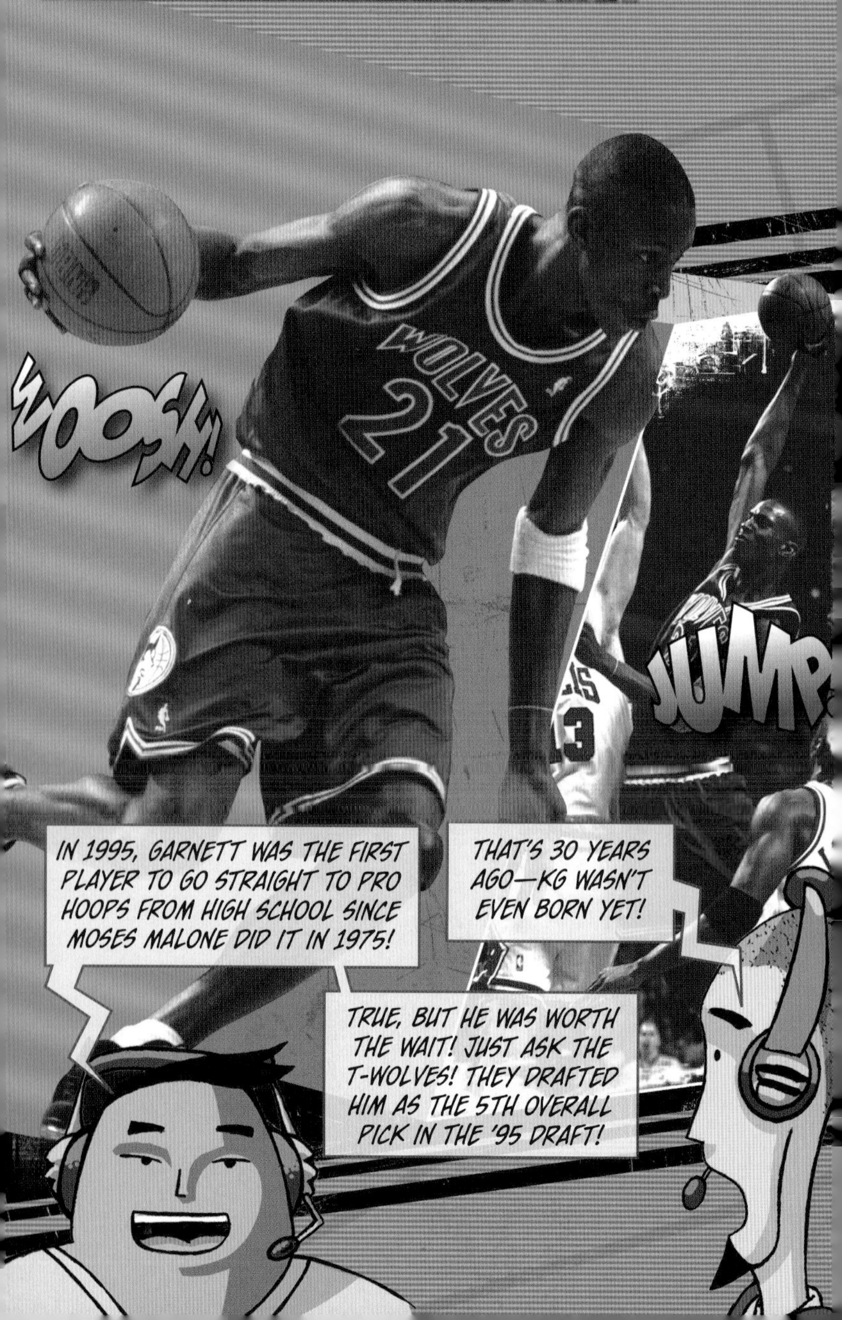
WOOSH!
JUMP
IN 1995, GARNETT WAS THE FIRST PLAYER TO GO STRAIGHT TO PRO HOOPS FROM HIGH SCHOOL SINCE MOSES MALONE DID IT IN 1975!
THAT'S 30 YEARS AGO—KG WASN'T EVEN BORN YET!
TRUE, BUT HE WAS WORTH THE WAIT! JUST ASK THE T-WOLVES! THEY DRAFTED HIM AS THE 5TH OVERALL PICK IN THE '95 DRAFT!

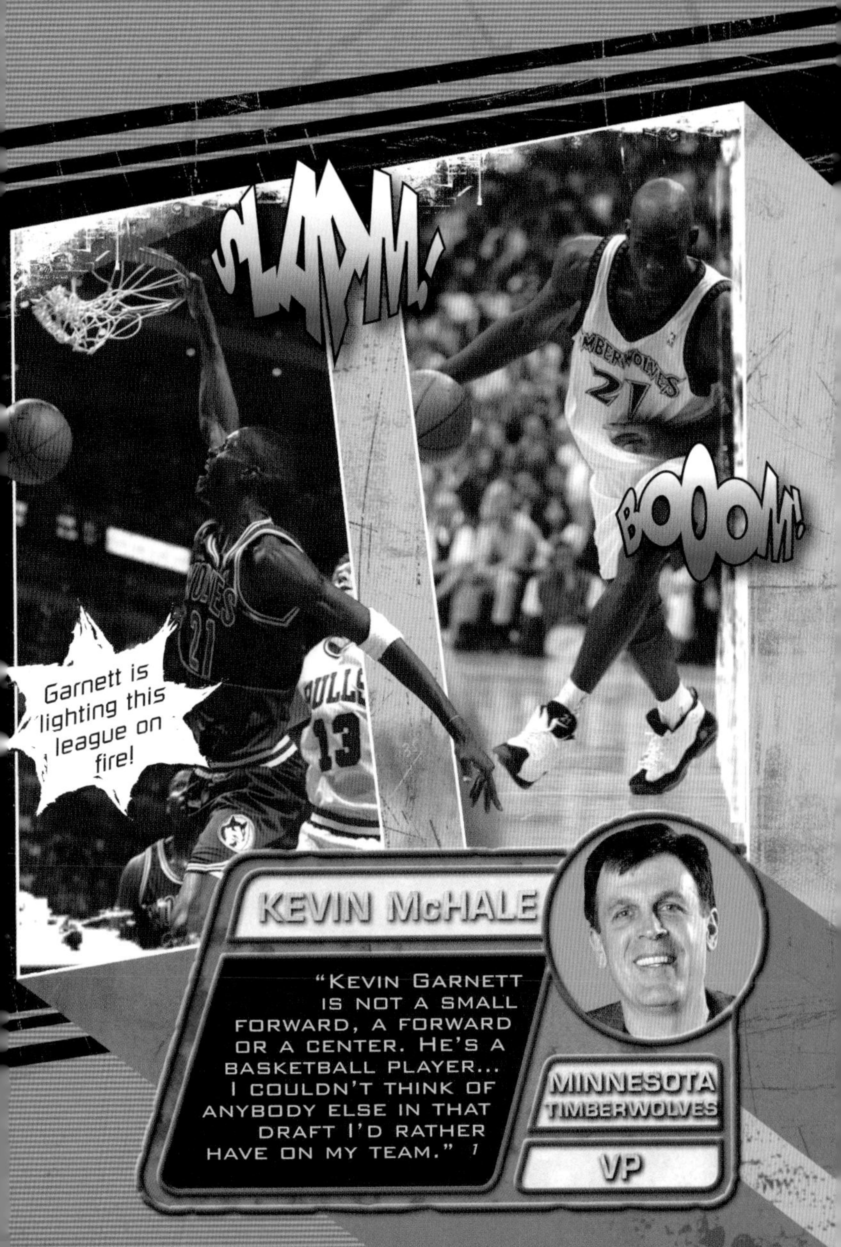
SLAM!
BOOOM!
Garnett is lighting this league on fire!
KEVIN McHALE
"KEVIN GARNETT IS NOT A SMALL FORWARD, A FORWARD OR A CENTER. HE'S A BASKETBALL PLAYER... I COULDN'T THINK OF ANYBODY ELSE IN THAT DRAFT I'D RATHER HAVE ON MY TEAM." [1]
MINNESOTA TIMBERWOLVES
VP

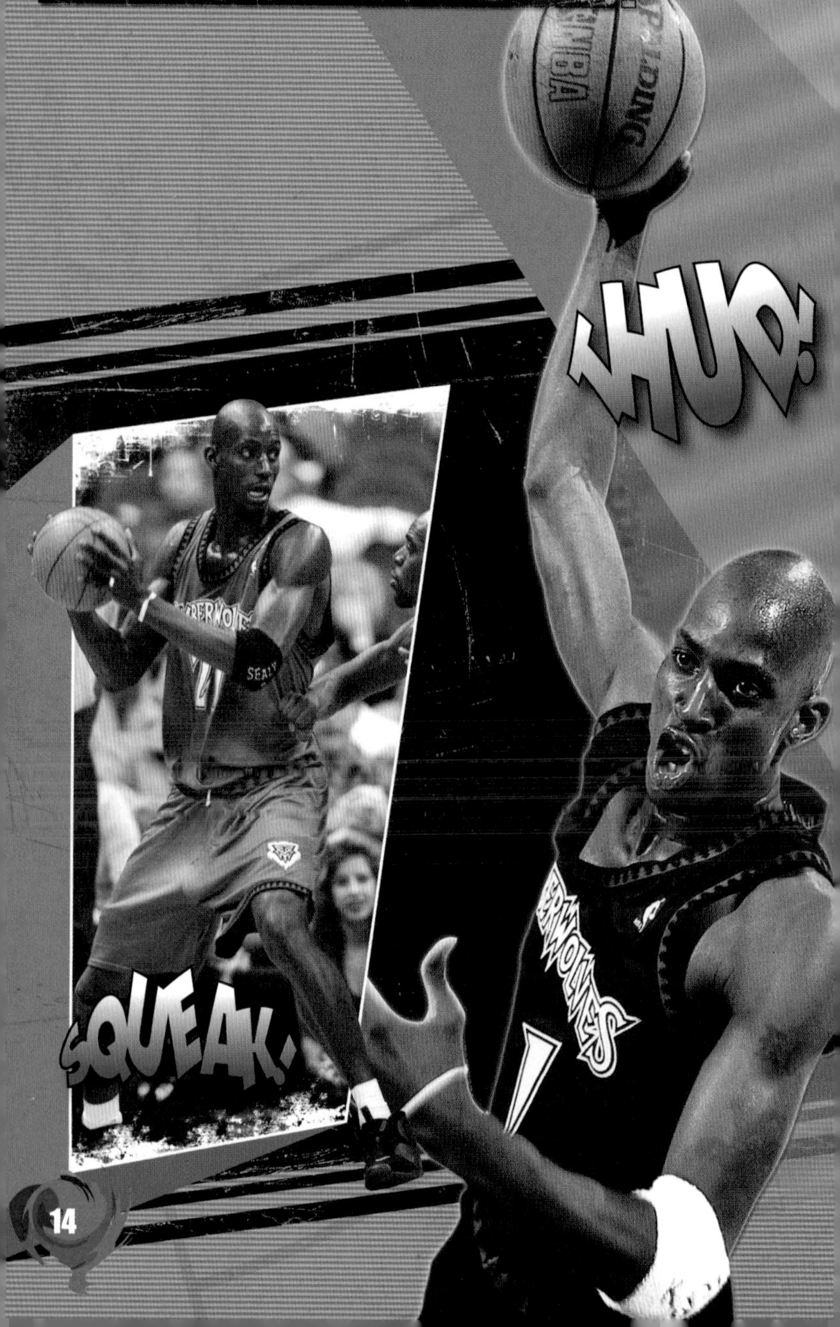
THUD!
SQUEAK!

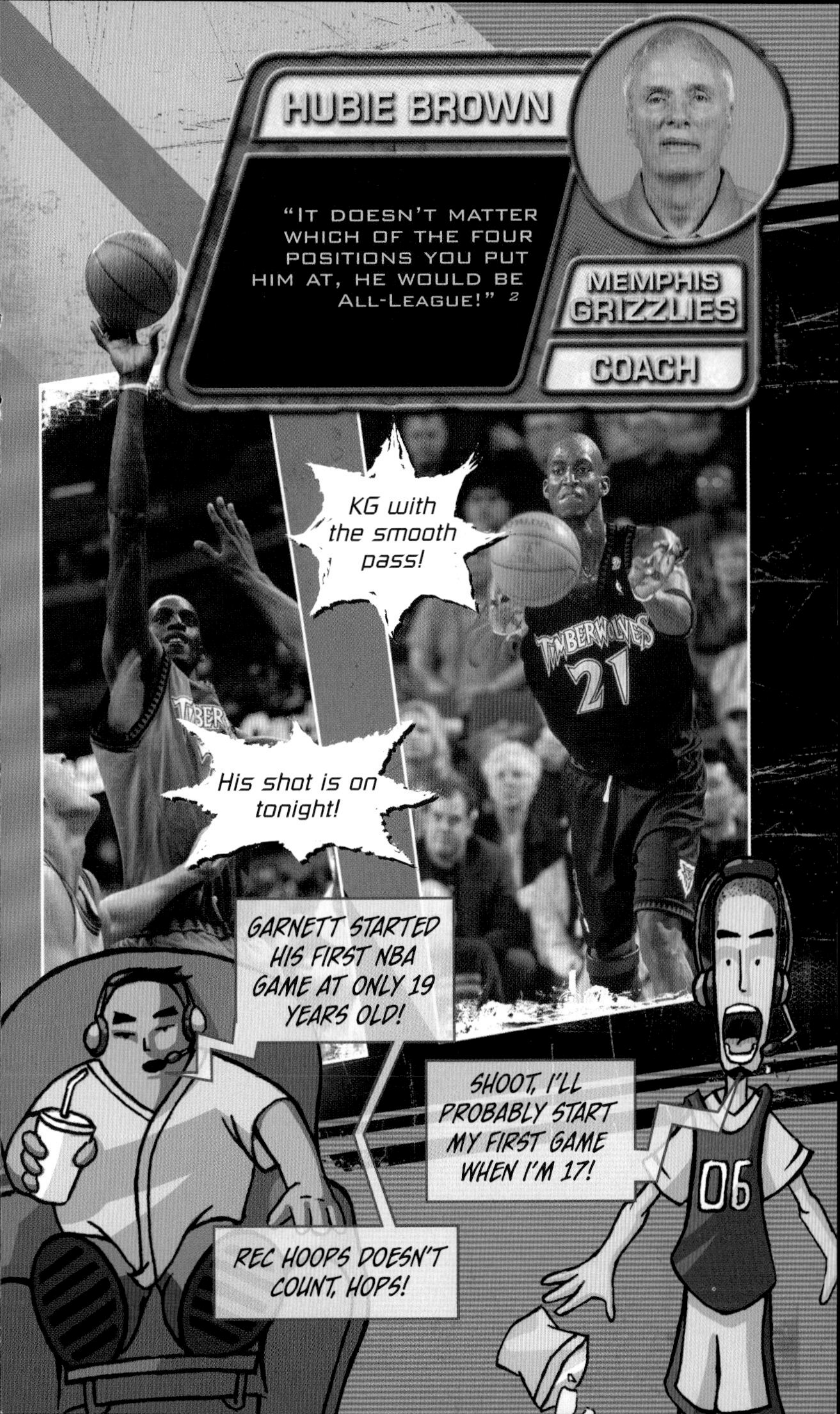
HUBIE BROWN
"IT DOESN'T MATTER WHICH OF THE FOUR POSITIONS YOU PUT HIM AT, HE WOULD BE ALL-LEAGUE!" [2]
MEMPHIS GRIZZLIES
COACH
KG with the smooth pass!
His shot is on tonight!
GARNETT STARTED HIS FIRST NBA GAME AT ONLY 19 YEARS OLD!
SHOOT, I'LL PROBABLY START MY FIRST GAME WHEN I'M 17!
REC HOOPS DOESN'T COUNT, HOPS!

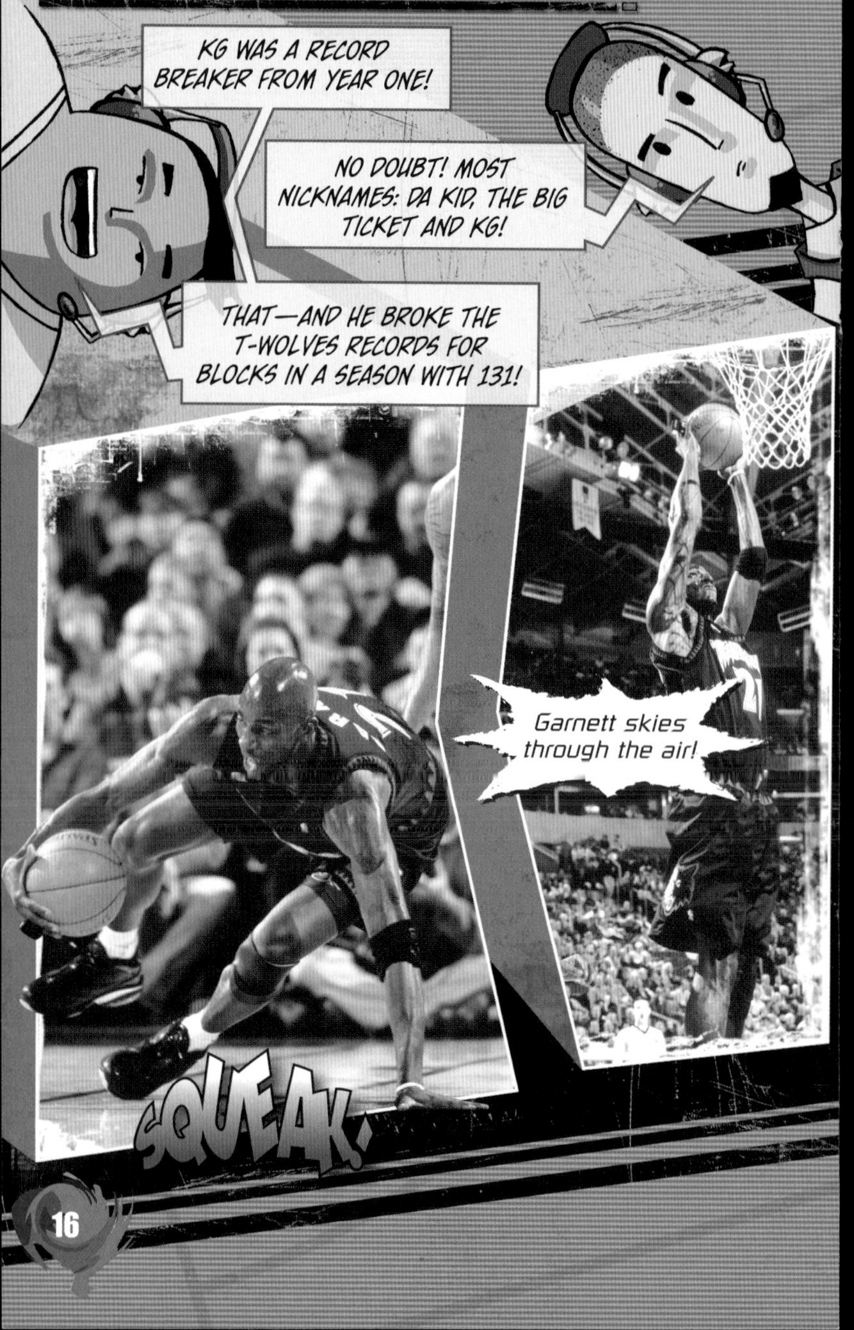
KG WAS A RECORD BREAKER FROM YEAR ONE!
NO DOUBT! MOST NICKNAMES: DA KID, THE BIG TICKET AND KG!
THAT—AND HE BROKE THE T-WOLVES RECORDS FOR BLOCKS IN A SEASON WITH 131!
Garnett skies through the air!
SQUEAK!

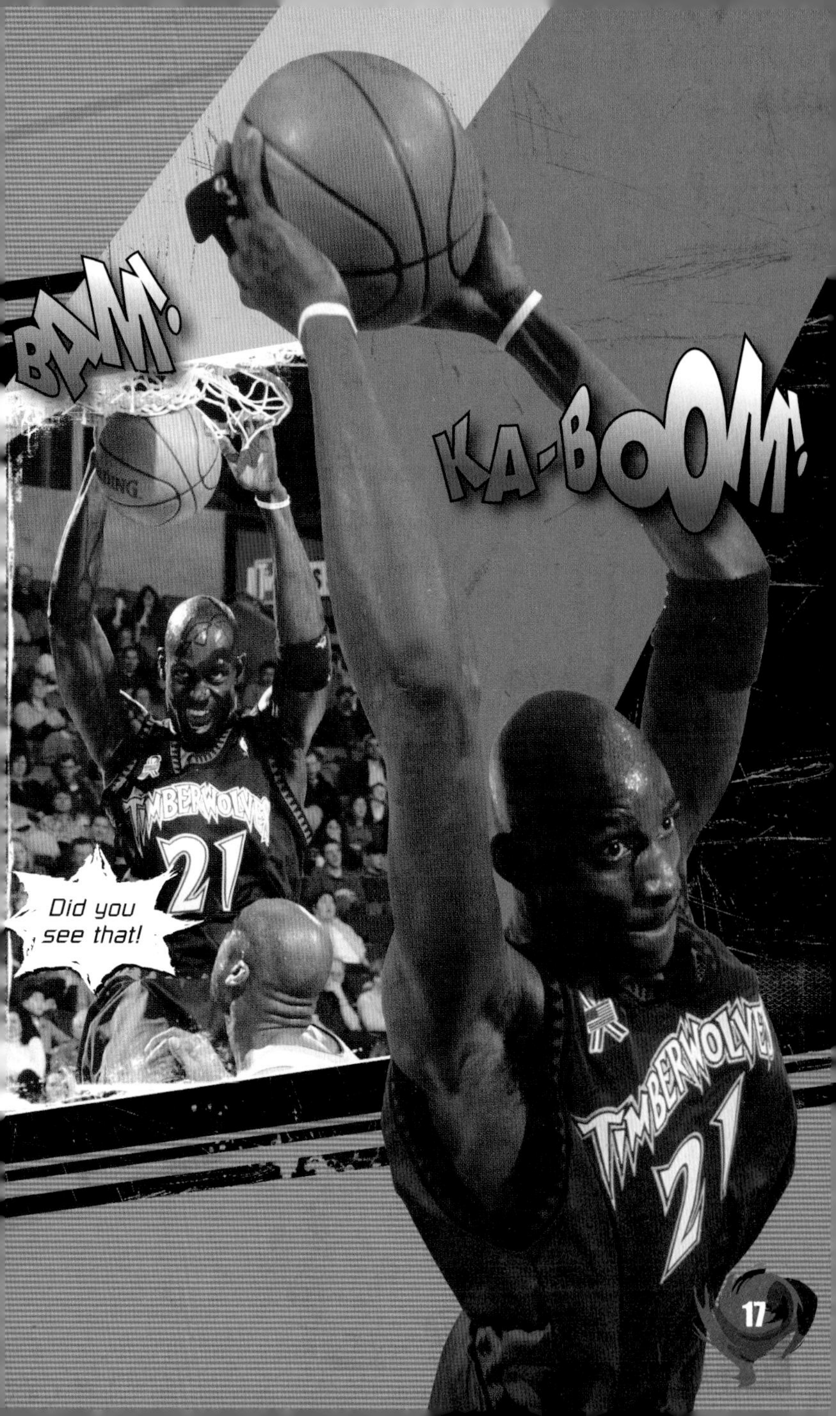
BAM!
KA-BOOM!
Did you see that!

skills

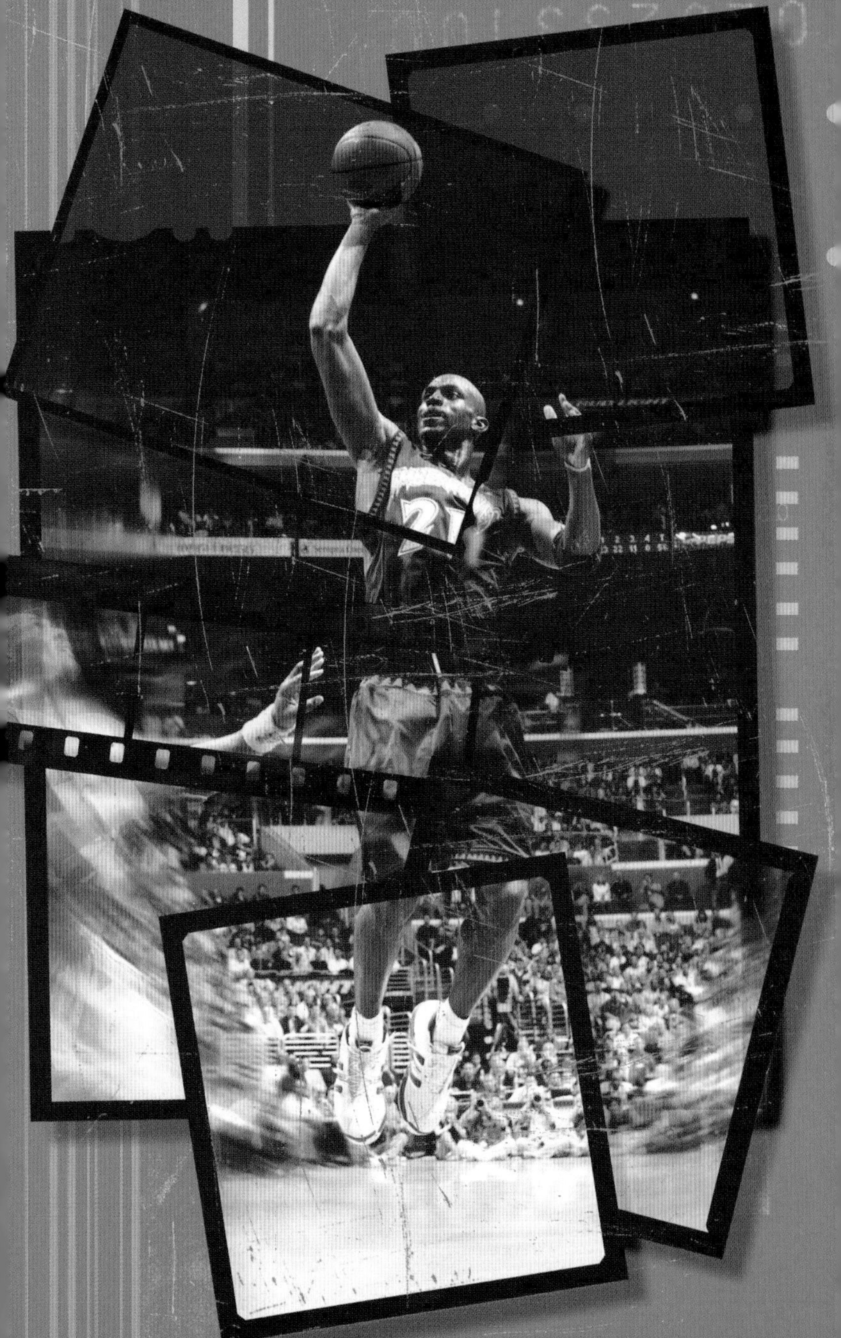

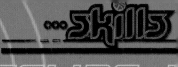

BASELINE J

BASELINE J

SHOT!

DRIVE BY
DEFENDER!

SQUARE
UP!

JUMP!

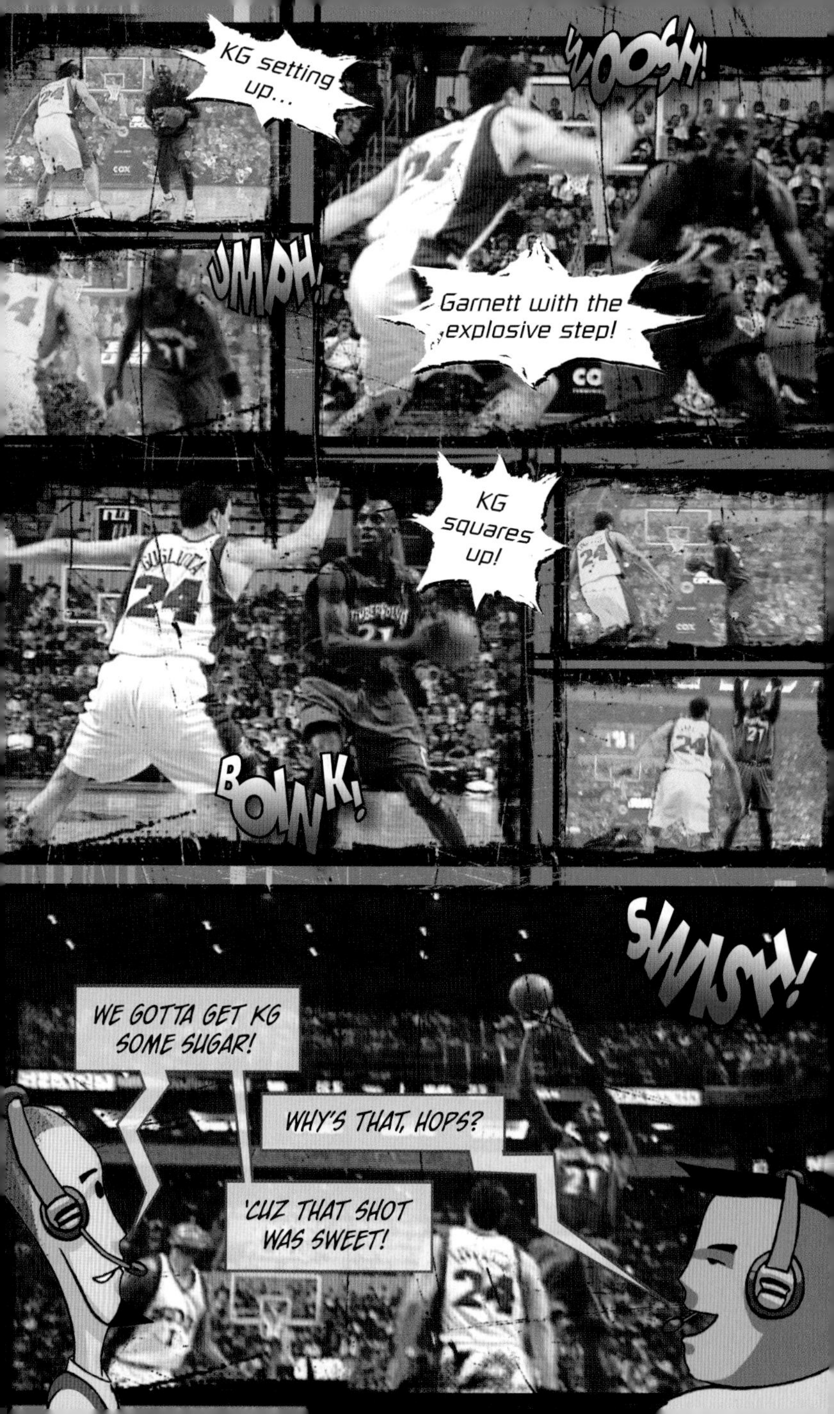
KG setting up...
WOOSH!
UMPH!
Garnett with the explosive step!
KG squares up!
BOINK!
SWISH!
WE GOTTA GET KG SOME SUGAR!
WHY'S THAT, HOPS?
'CUZ THAT SHOT WAS SWEET!

DRIVING TO THE BASKET

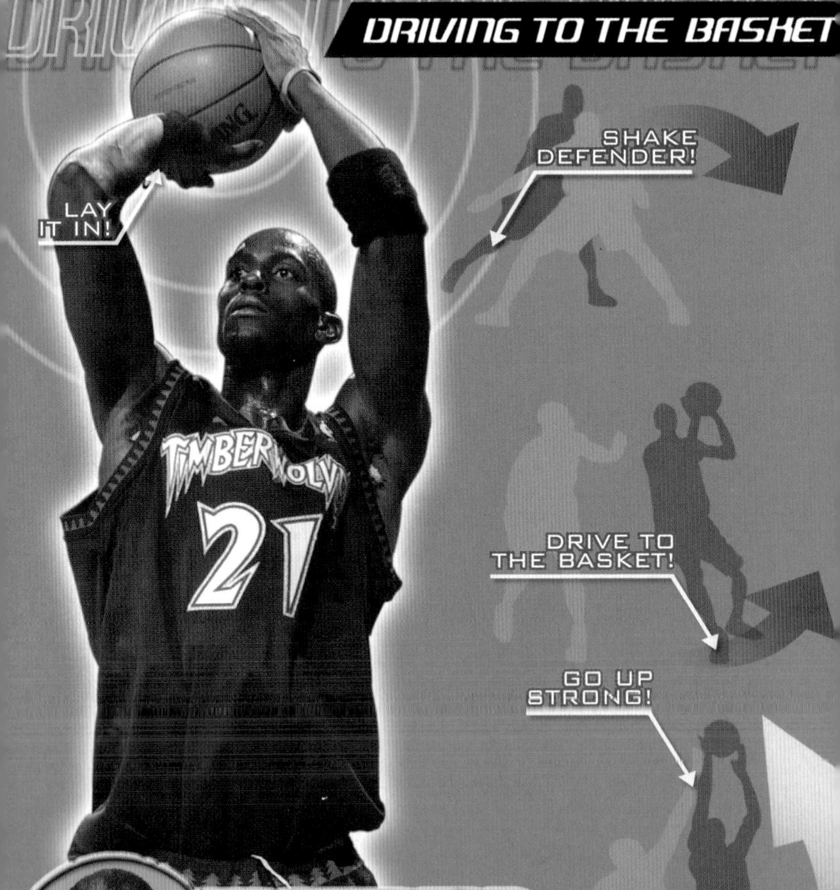
SHAKE DEFENDER!
LAY IT IN!
DRIVE TO THE BASKET!
GO UP STRONG!

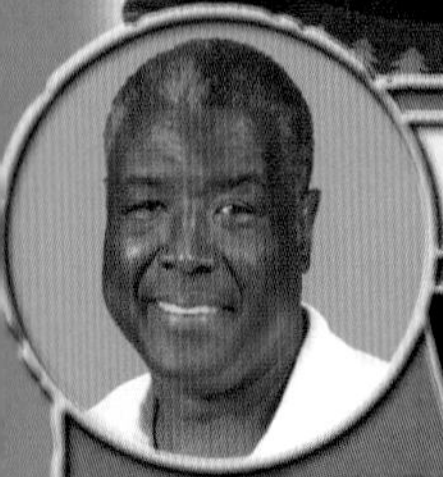

PAUL SILAS

CLEVELAND CAVALIERS

COACH

"GOING BACK 40 YEARS, I CAN'T REALLY THINK OF ANYBODY THAT CAN DO ALL THE THINGS GARNETT CAN DO." [3]

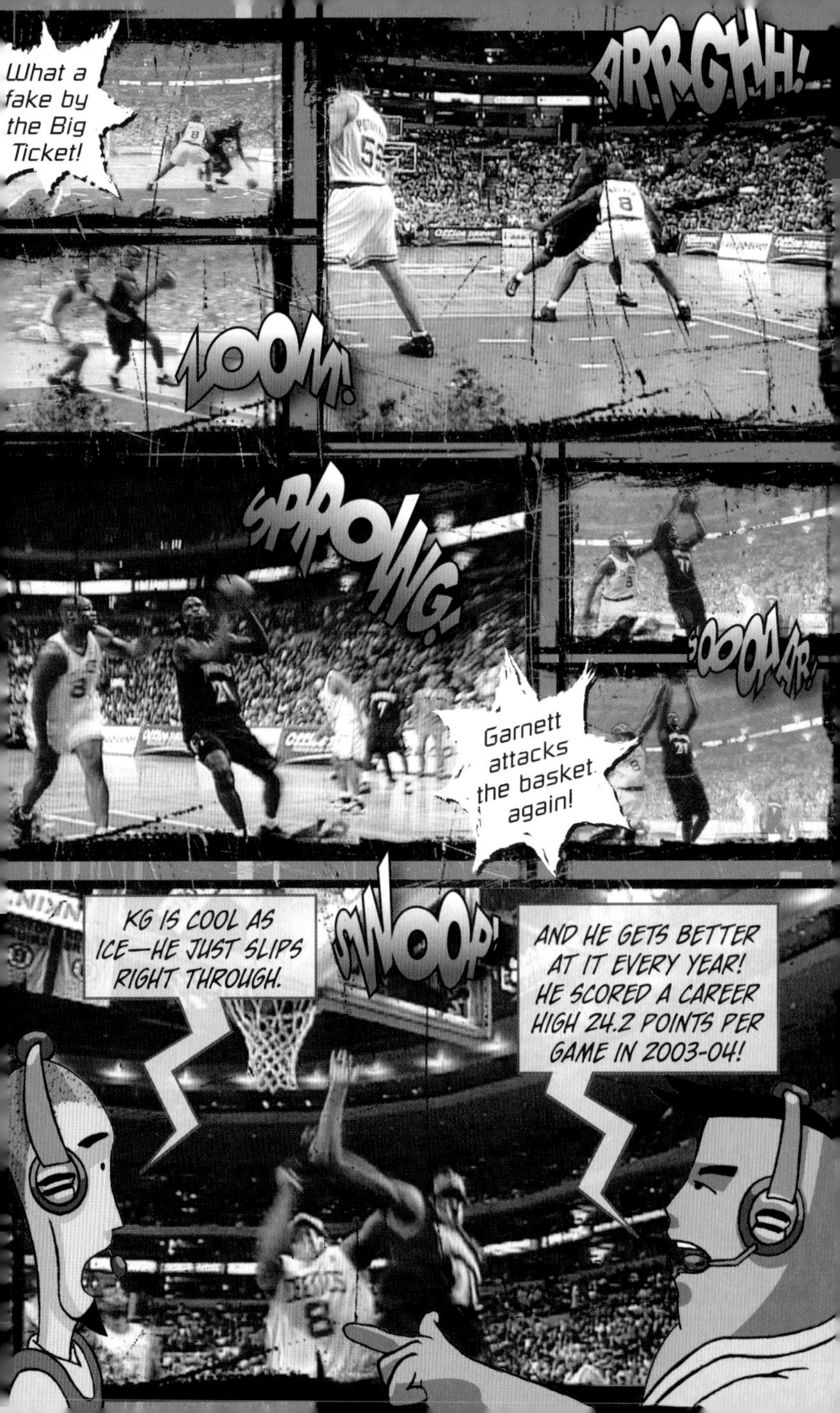
What a fake by the Big Ticket!
ARRGHH!
ZOOM!
SPROING!
Garnett attacks the basket again!
KG IS COOL AS ICE—HE JUST SLIPS RIGHT THROUGH.
SWOOP!
AND HE GETS BETTER AT IT EVERY YEAR! HE SCORED A CAREER HIGH 24.2 POINTS PER GAME IN 2003-04!

...skills

POSTING UP

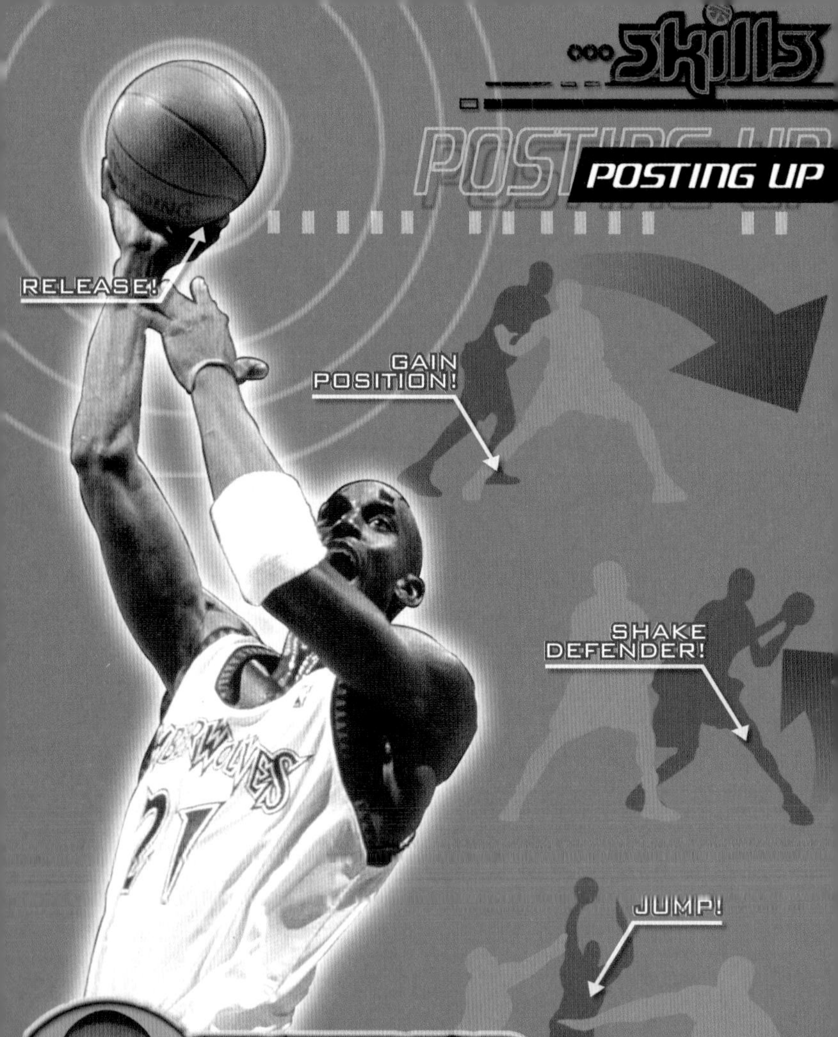

RELEASE!
GAIN POSITION!
SHAKE DEFENDER!
JUMP!

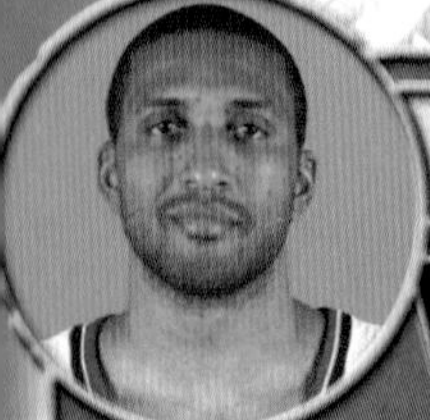

SHAREEF ABDUR-RAHIM

PORTLAND TRAILBLAZERS

FORWARD

"HE JUST GETS BETTER EVERY YEAR. HE'S PLAYING BETTER THAN ANYBODY RIGHT NOW." [4]

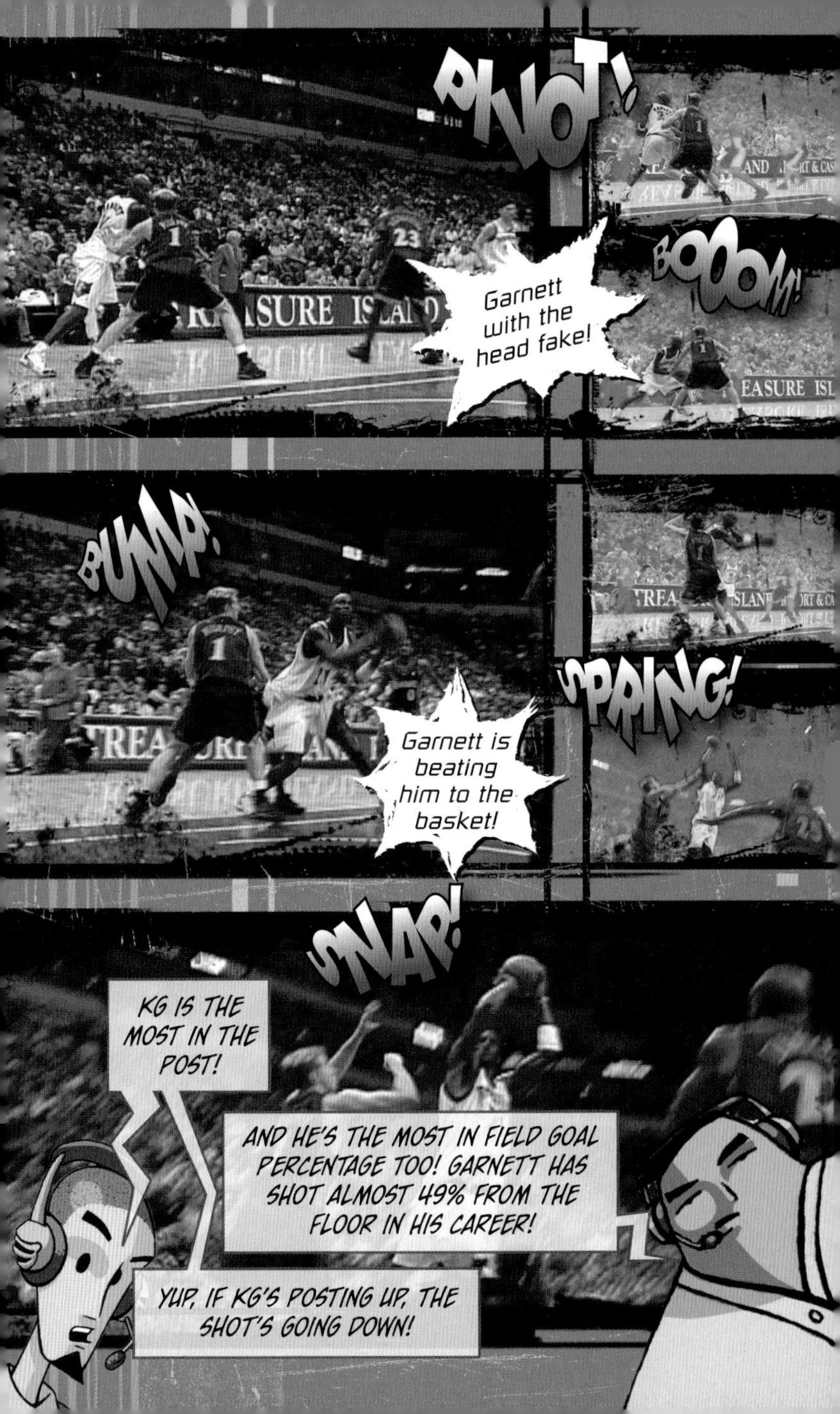
PIVOT!
Garnett with the head fake!
BOOOM!
BUMP!
Garnett is beating him to the basket!
SPRING!
SNAP!
KG IS THE MOST IN THE POST!
AND HE'S THE MOST IN FIELD GOAL PERCENTAGE TOO! GARNETT HAS SHOT ALMOST 49% FROM THE FLOOR IN HIS CAREER!
YUP, IF KG'S POSTING UP, THE SHOT'S GOING DOWN!

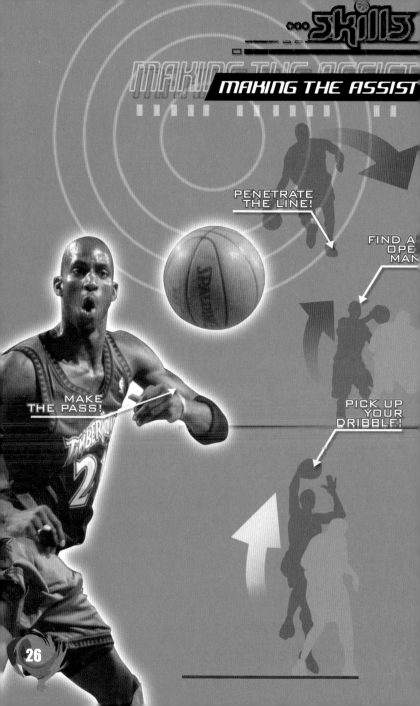

MAKING THE ASSIST

PENETRATE THE LINE!

FIND A OPE MAN

MAKE THE PASS!

PICK UP YOUR DRIBBLE!

26

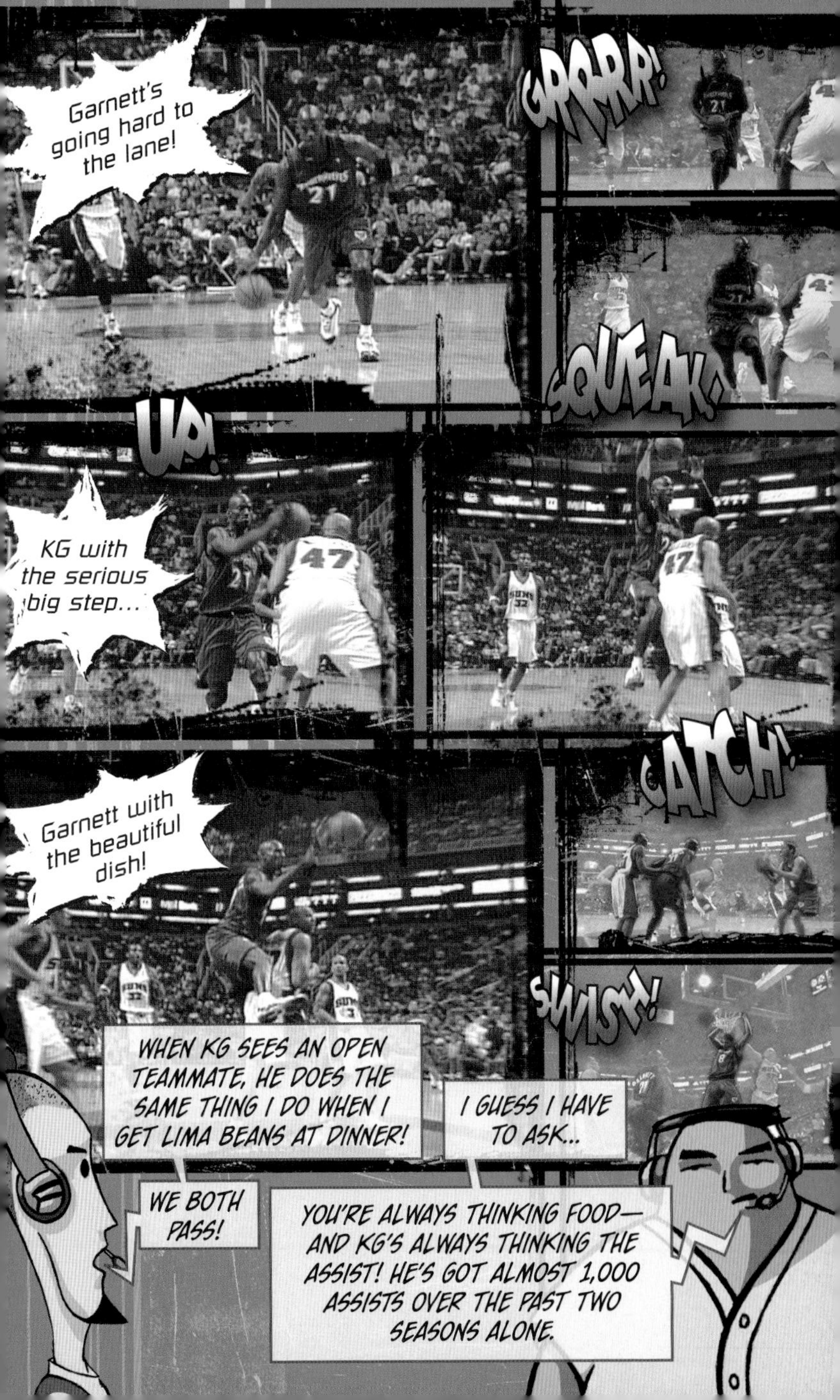

Garnett's going hard to the lane!
GRRRR!
SQUEAK!
UP!
KG with the serious big step...
Garnett with the beautiful dish!
CATCH!
SWISH!
WHEN KG SEES AN OPEN TEAMMATE, HE DOES THE SAME THING I DO WHEN I GET LIMA BEANS AT DINNER!
I GUESS I HAVE TO ASK...
WE BOTH PASS!
YOU'RE ALWAYS THINKING FOOD— AND KG'S ALWAYS THINKING THE ASSIST! HE'S GOT ALMOST 1,000 ASSISTS OVER THE PAST TWO SEASONS ALONE.

TOUGH DEFENSE

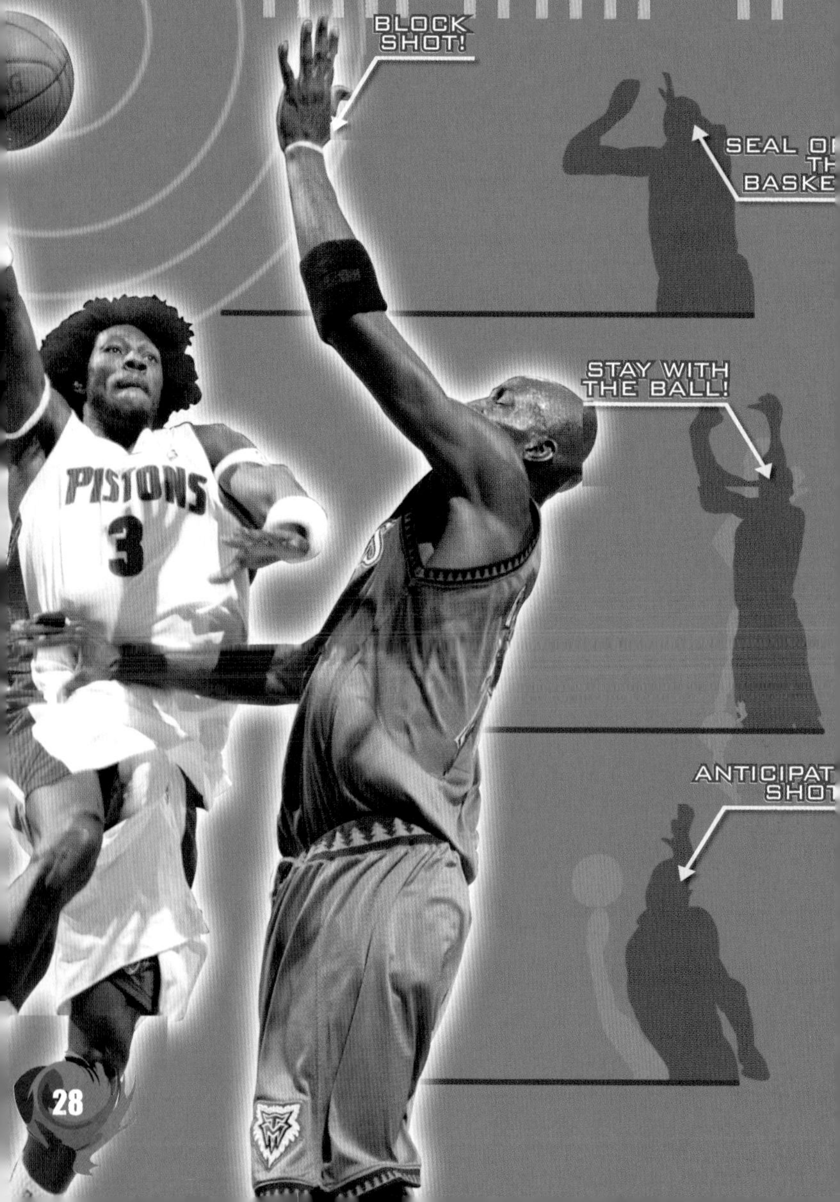
BLOCK SHOT!
SEAL O
TH
BASKE
STAY WITH THE BALL!
ANTICIPAT
SHOT
PISTONS
3

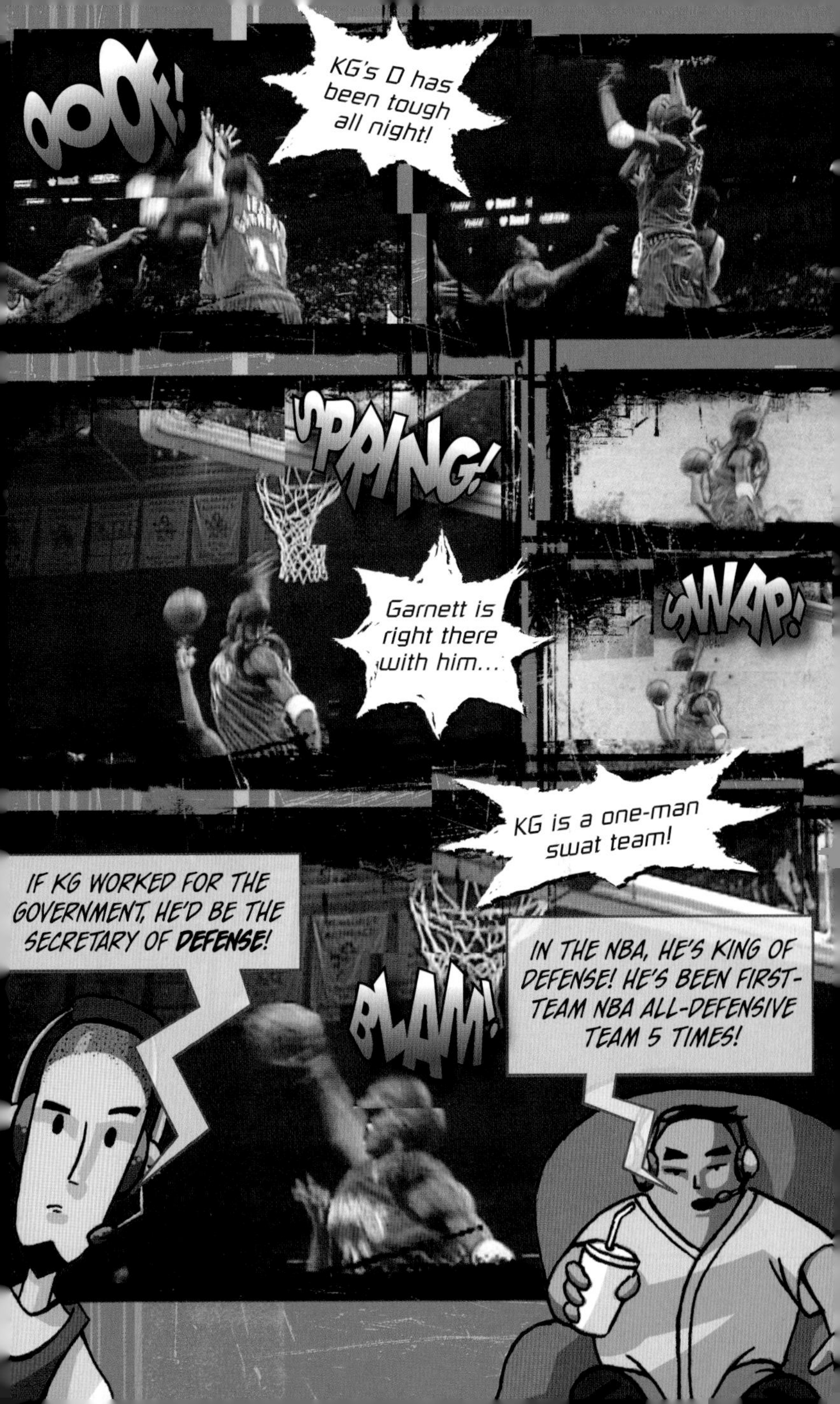
OOOF!
KG's D has been tough all night!
SPRING!
Garnett is right there with him...
SNAP!
KG is a one-man swat team!
IF KG WORKED FOR THE GOVERNMENT, HE'D BE THE SECRETARY OF DEFENSE!
BLAM!
IN THE NBA, HE'S KING OF DEFENSE! HE'S BEEN FIRST-TEAM NBA ALL-DEFENSIVE TEAM 5 TIMES!

COAST TO COAST

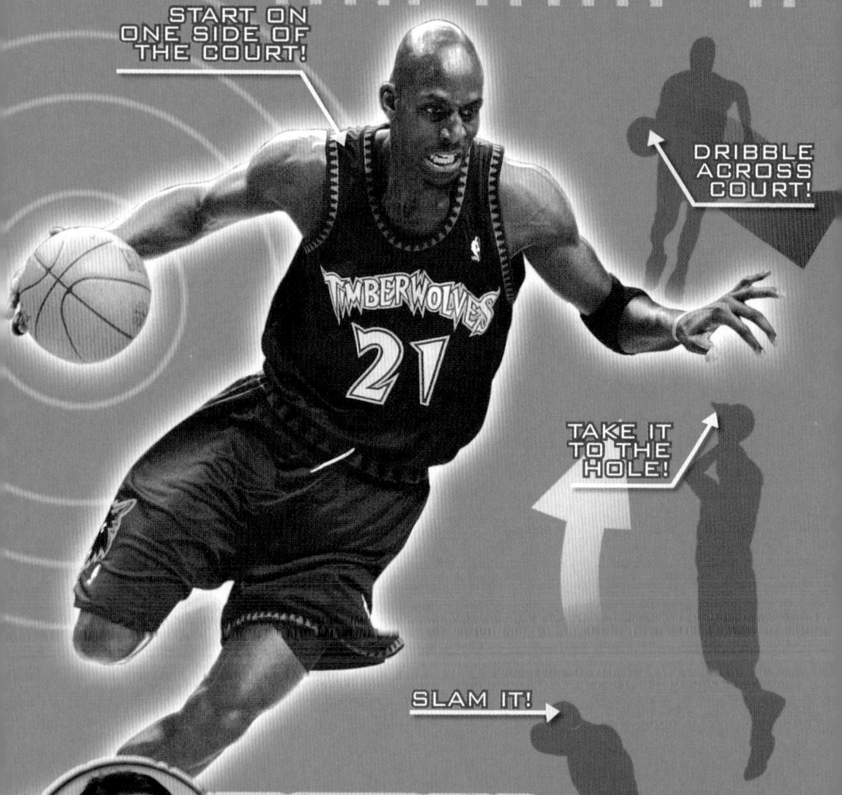
START ON ONE SIDE OF THE COURT!
DRIBBLE ACROSS COURT!
TAKE IT TO THE HOLE!
SLAM IT!

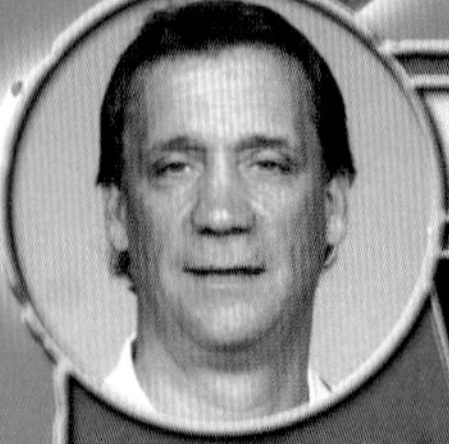

FLIP SAUNDERS

MINNESOTA TIMBERWOLVES

COACH

"PEOPLE ARE STARTING TO UNDERSTAND, HE'S A 6-5 PLAYER IN A 7-1 FRAME. EVEN IF YOU JUST WATCH HIM RUN, HIS FEET HIT THE FLOOR AND YOU DON'T EVEN HEAR IT."[5]

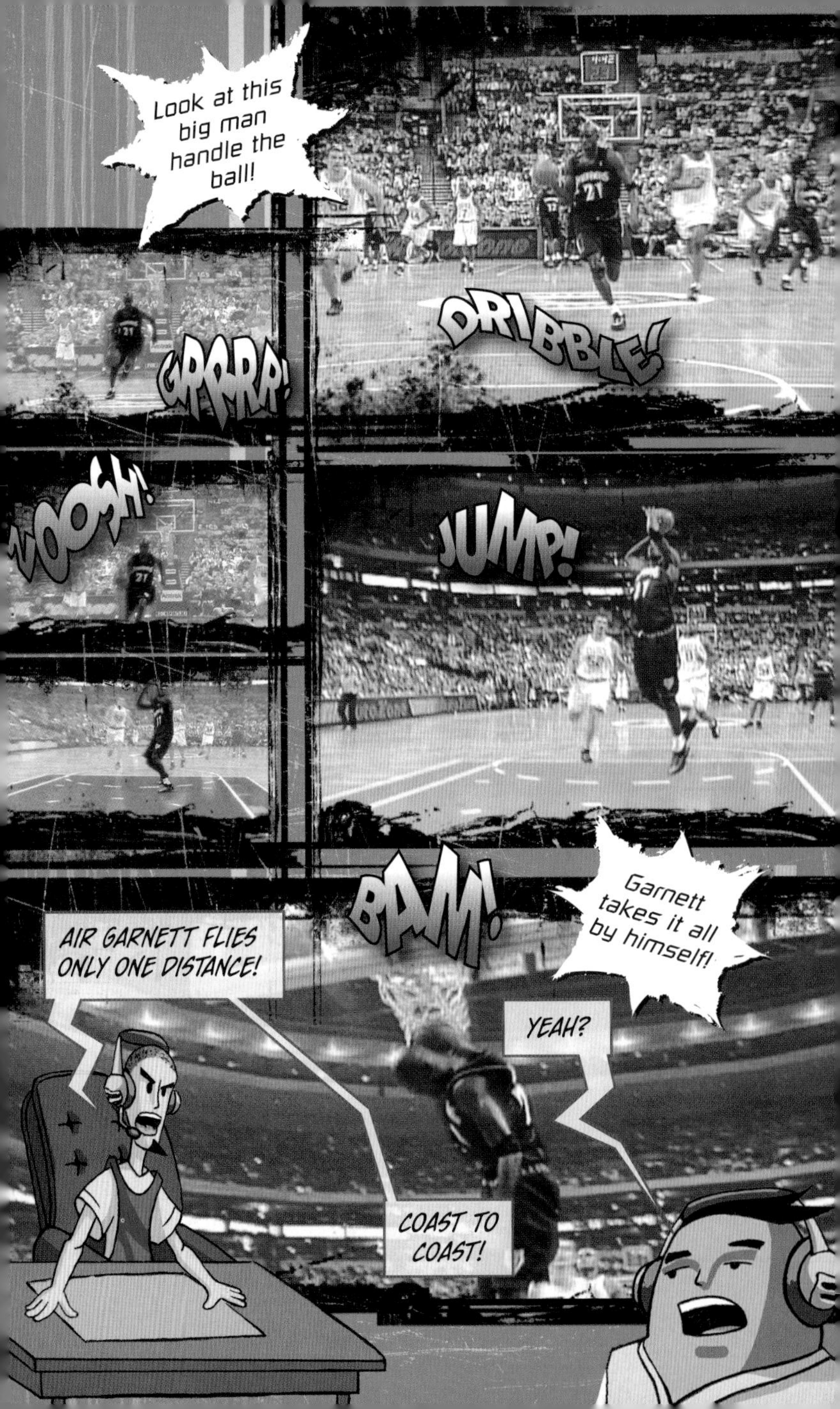
Look at this big man handle the ball!
GRRRR!
DRIBBLE!
WOOSH!
JUMP!
BAM!
Garnett takes it all by himself!
AIR GARNETT FLIES ONLY ONE DISTANCE!
YEAH?
COAST TO COAST!

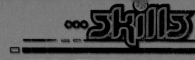

BLOCKING

BLOCK
THE
SHOT!

STAY
ON
YOUR
MAN!

KEEP YOU
EYE O
THE BAL

PUT YOUR
ARM UP!

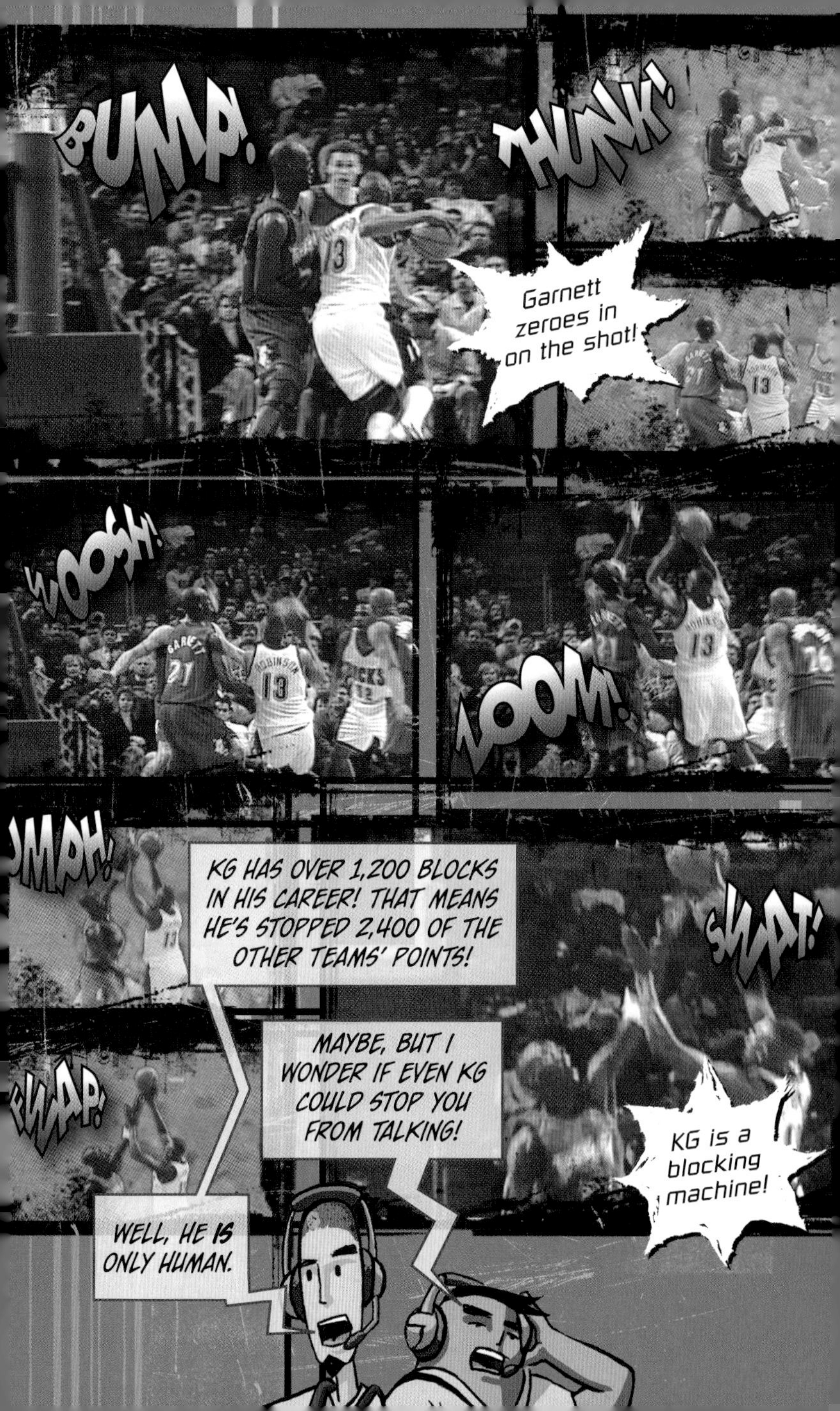
BUMP!
THUNK!
Garnett zeroes in on the shot!
WOOSH!
ZOOM!
MPH!
KG HAS OVER 1,200 BLOCKS IN HIS CAREER! THAT MEANS HE'S STOPPED 2,400 OF THE OTHER TEAMS' POINTS!
SWAT!
WAP!
MAYBE, BUT I WONDER IF EVEN KG COULD STOP YOU FROM TALKING!
KG is a blocking machine!
WELL, HE *IS* ONLY HUMAN.

WINGSPAN

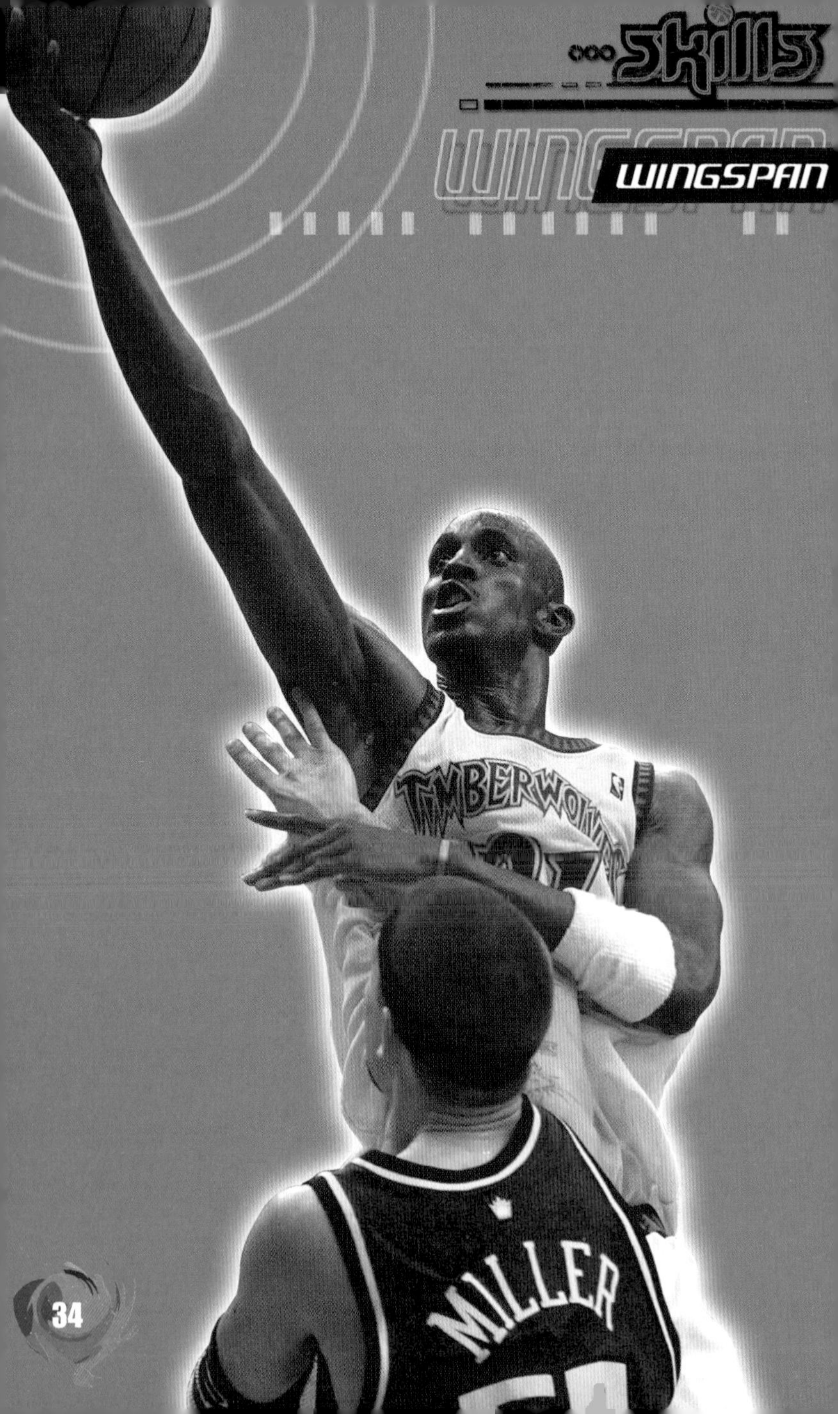
TIMBERWOLVES
MILLER

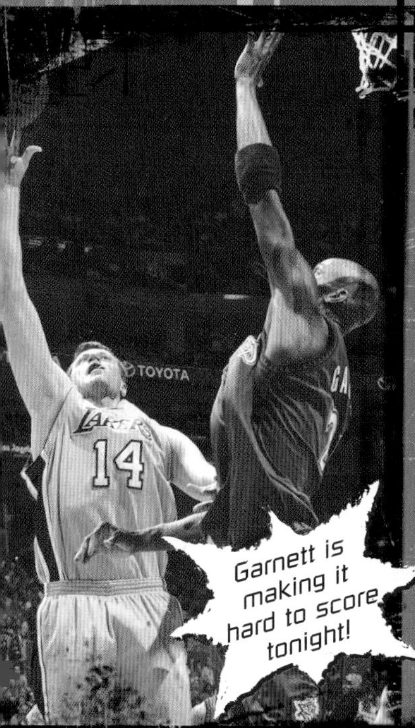

Garnett is making it hard to score tonight!

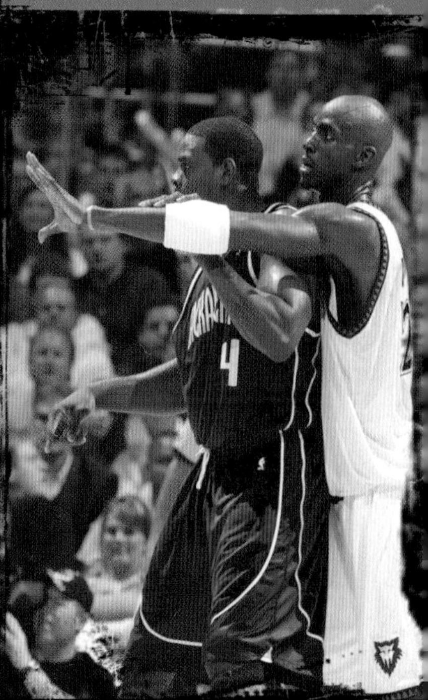

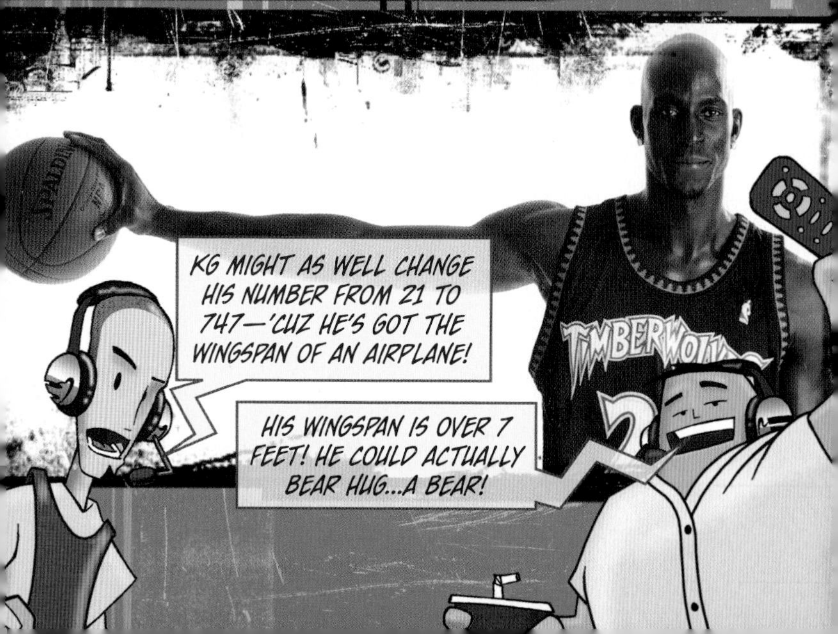

KG MIGHT AS WELL CHANGE HIS NUMBER FROM 21 TO 747—'CUZ HE'S GOT THE WINGSPAN OF AN AIRPLANE!
HIS WINGSPAN IS OVER 7 FEET! HE COULD ACTUALLY BEAR HUG...A BEAR!

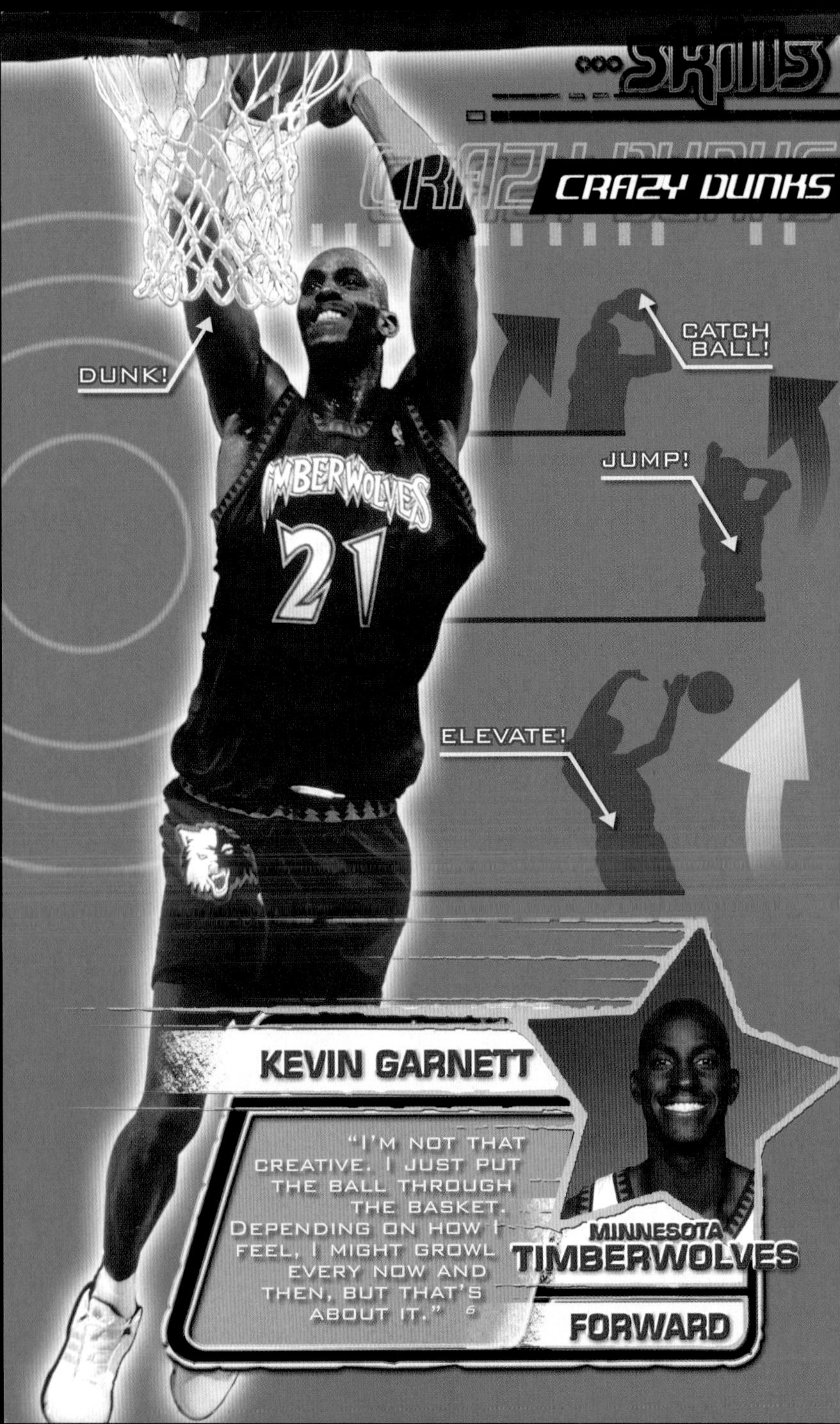
SKILLS
CRAZY DUNKS
CATCH BALL!
DUNK!
JUMP!
ELEVATE!
KEVIN GARNETT
"I'M NOT THAT CREATIVE. I JUST PUT THE BALL THROUGH THE BASKET. DEPENDING ON HOW I FEEL, I MIGHT GROWL EVERY NOW AND THEN, BUT THAT'S ABOUT IT." 6
MINNESOTA TIMBERWOLVES
FORWARD

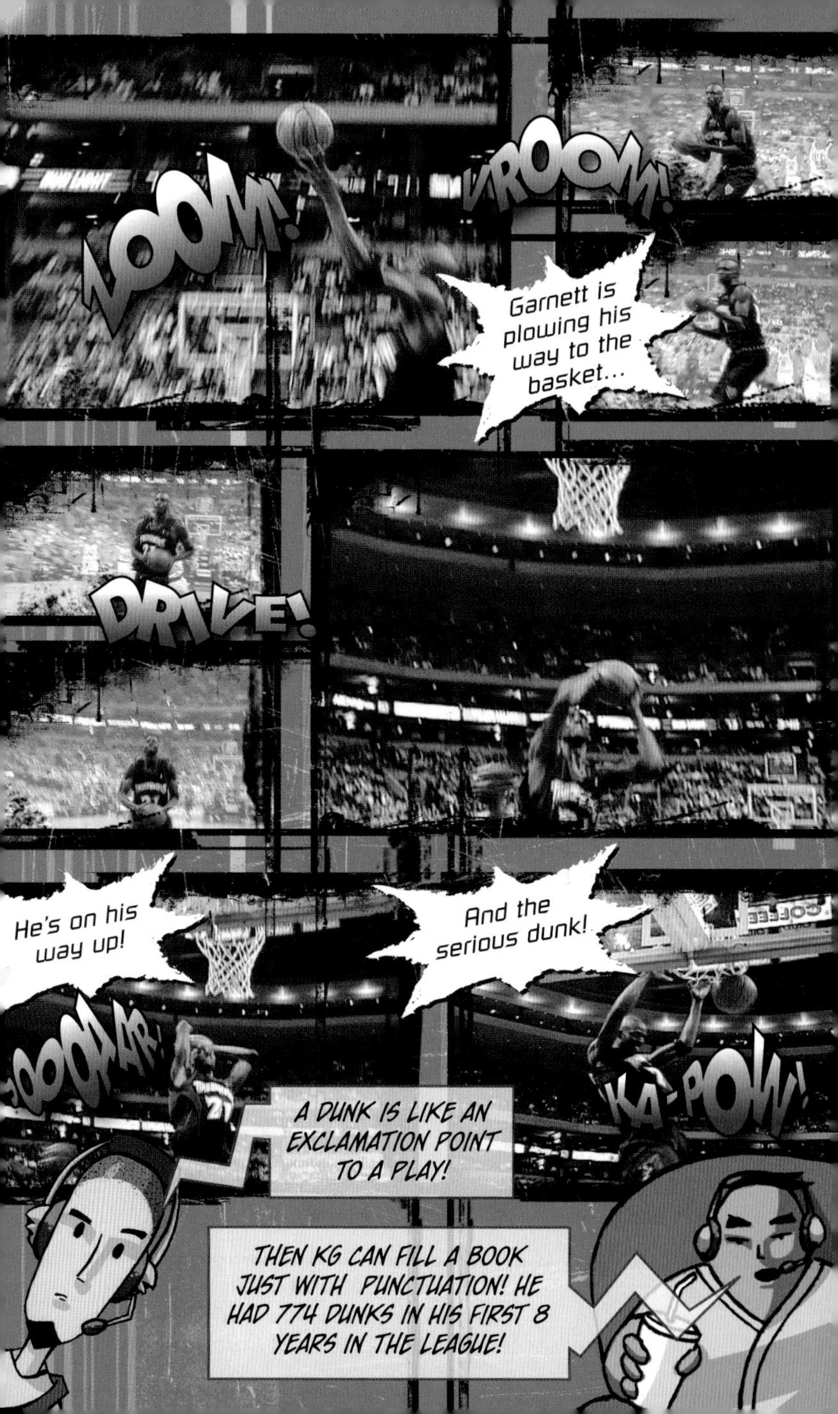

ZOOM!
VROOM!
Garnett is plowing his way to the basket...
DRIVE!
He's on his way up!
And the serious dunk!
KA-POW!
A DUNK IS LIKE AN EXCLAMATION POINT TO A PLAY!
THEN KG CAN FILL A BOOK JUST WITH PUNCTUATION! HE HAD 774 DUNKS IN HIS FIRST 8 YEARS IN THE LEAGUE!

greatest moments

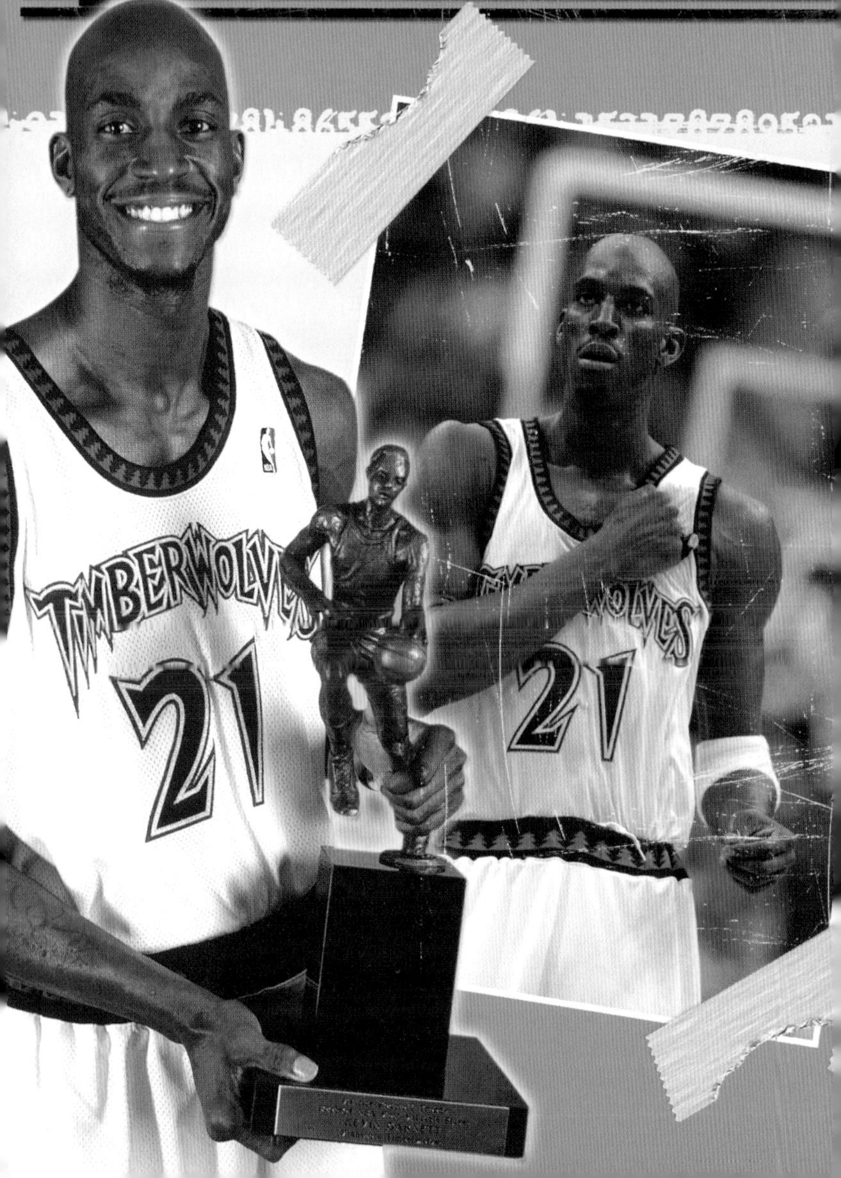
TIMBERWOLVES
21
TIMBERWOLVES
21

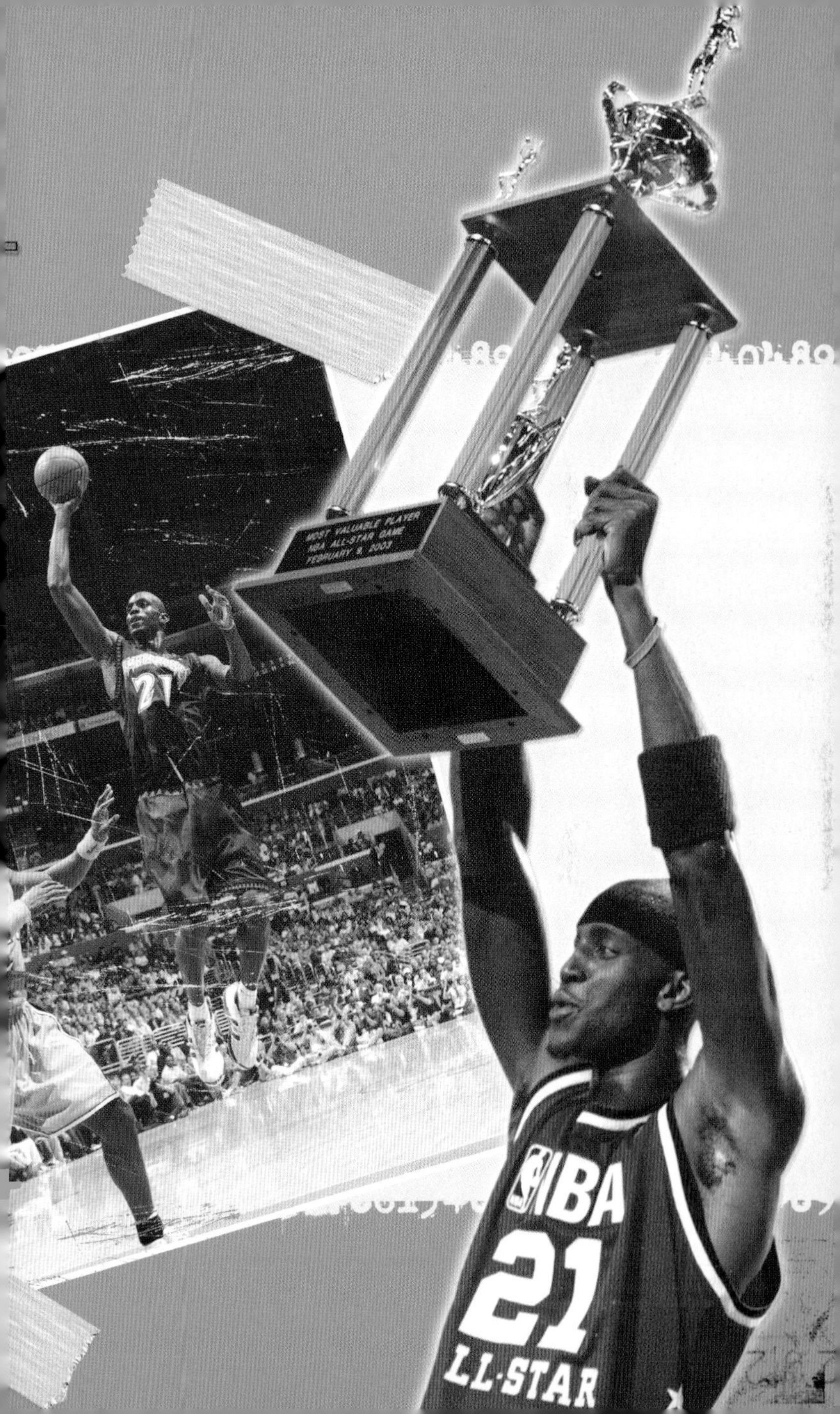
MOST VALUABLE PLAYER
NBA ALL-STAR GAME
FEBRUARY 9, 2003
NBA
21
LL-STAR

February 9, 2003: 2003 All-Star MVP

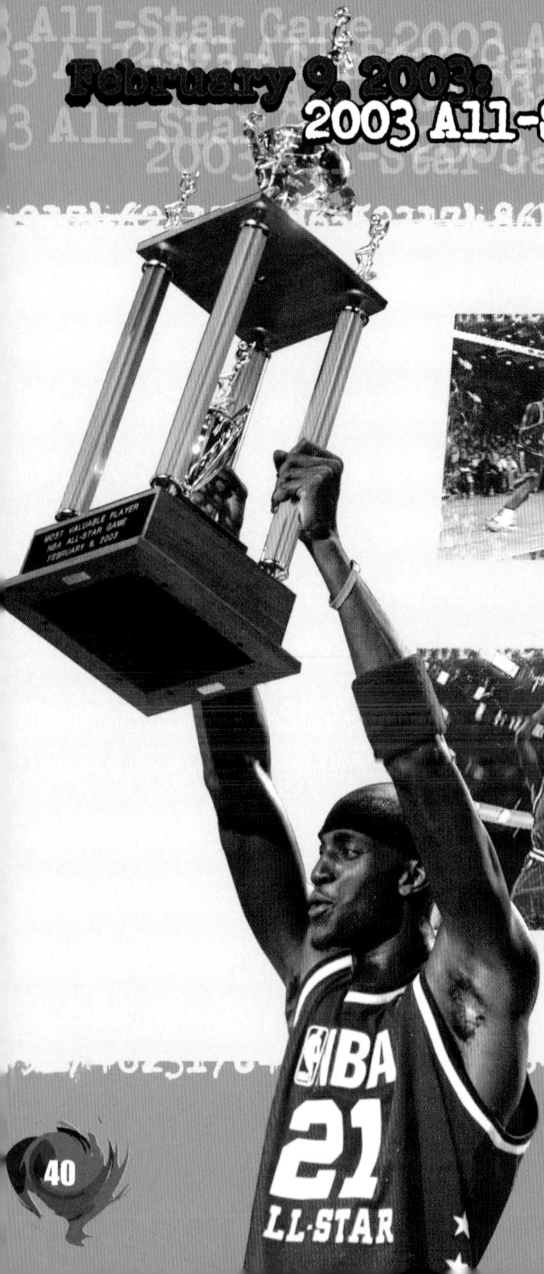
MOST VALUABLE PLAYER
NBA ALL-STAR GAME
FEBRUARY 9, 2003

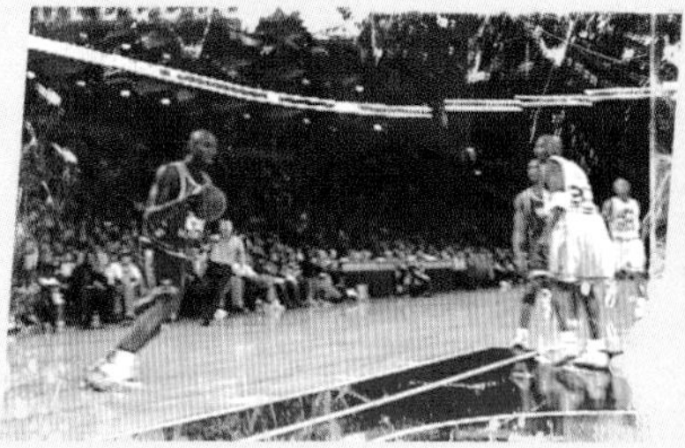

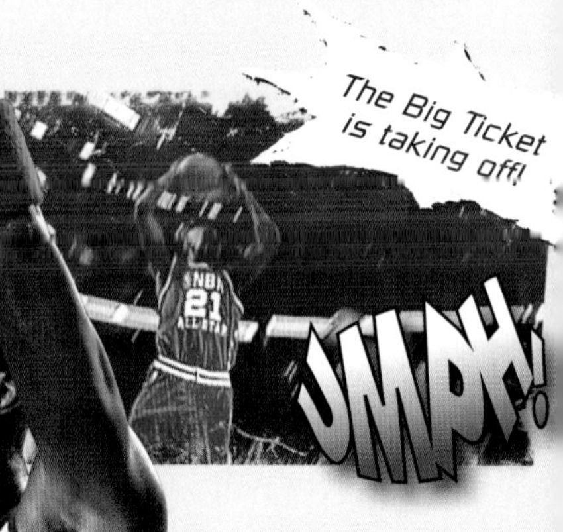
The Big Ticket is taking off!
UMPH!

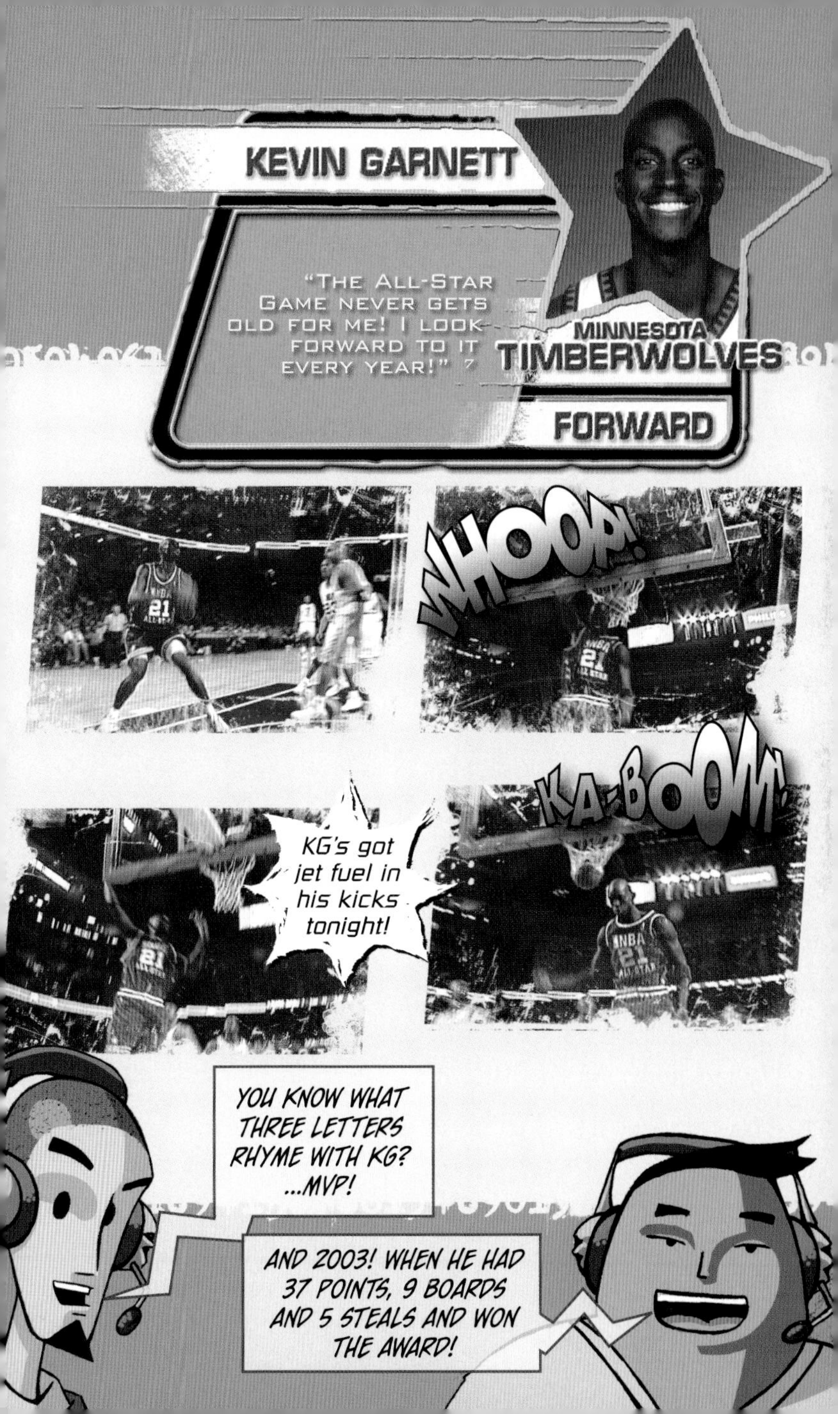
KEVIN GARNETT
"THE ALL-STAR GAME NEVER GETS OLD FOR ME! I LOOK FORWARD TO IT EVERY YEAR!" [7]
MINNESOTA TIMBERWOLVES
FORWARD
WHOOP!
KG's got jet fuel in his kicks tonight!
KA-BOOM!
YOU KNOW WHAT THREE LETTERS RHYME WITH KG? ...MVP!
AND 2003! WHEN HE HAD 37 POINTS, 9 BOARDS AND 5 STEALS AND WON THE AWARD!

greatest moments

March 22, 2000:
40 Points in Bean Town!

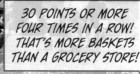

And KG spins away from the Boston defenders!

YOU KNOW, HOPS, THIS 40-POINT GAME WAS THE KID'S FOURTH STRAIGHT GAME WITH 30+ POINTS!

30 POINTS OR MORE FOUR TIMES IN A ROW! THAT'S MORE BASKETS THAN A GROCERY STORE!

DANG, HOPS. WE'LL EAT LUNCH AT THE END OF THE GAME, ALL RIGHT?!

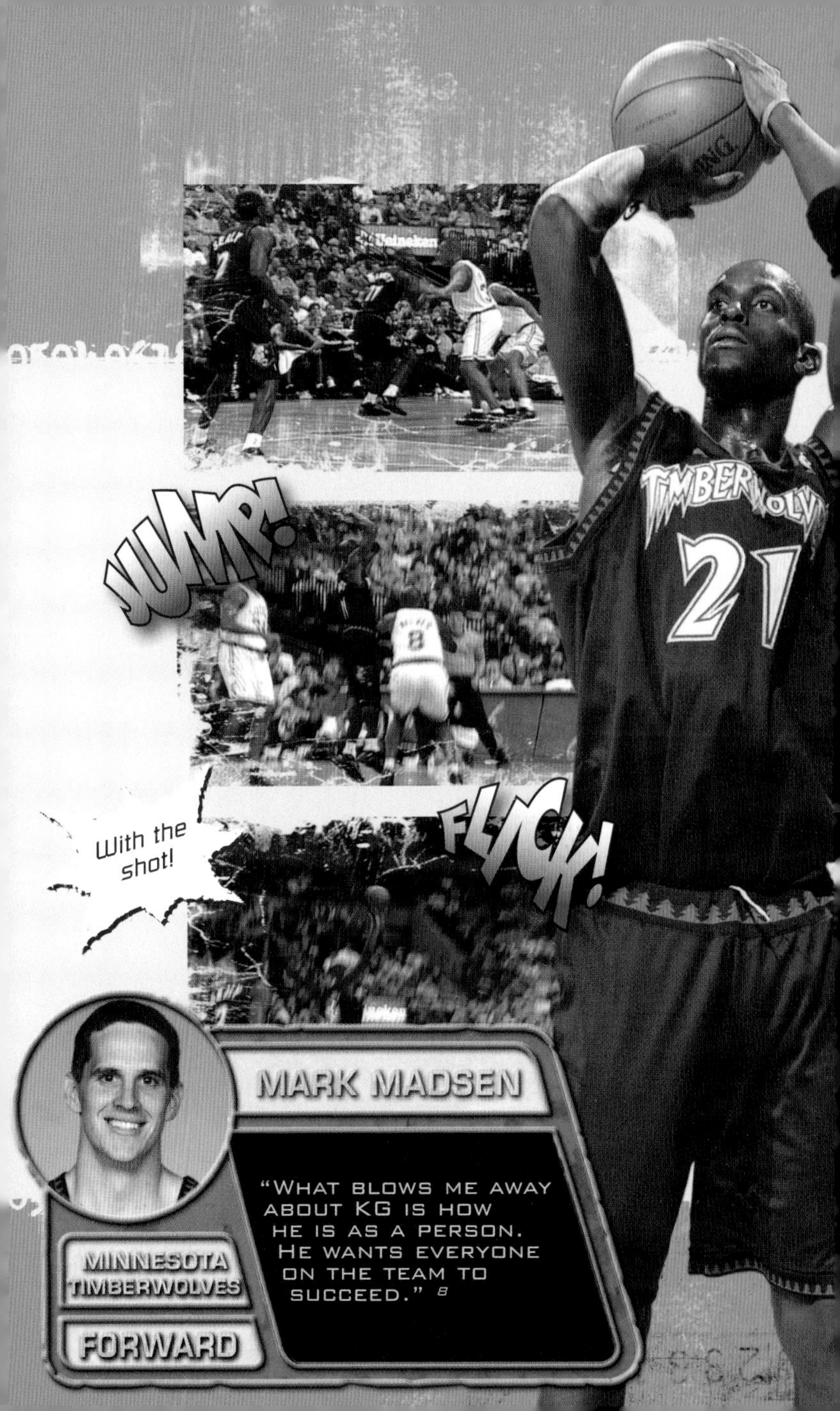
JUMP!
With the shot!
FLICK!
MARK MADSEN
MINNESOTA TIMBERWOLVES
FORWARD
"WHAT BLOWS ME AWAY ABOUT KG IS HOW HE IS AS A PERSON. HE WANTS EVERYONE ON THE TEAM TO SUCCEED." [8]

March 30, 1999: Almost Perfect FGP vs. Dallas

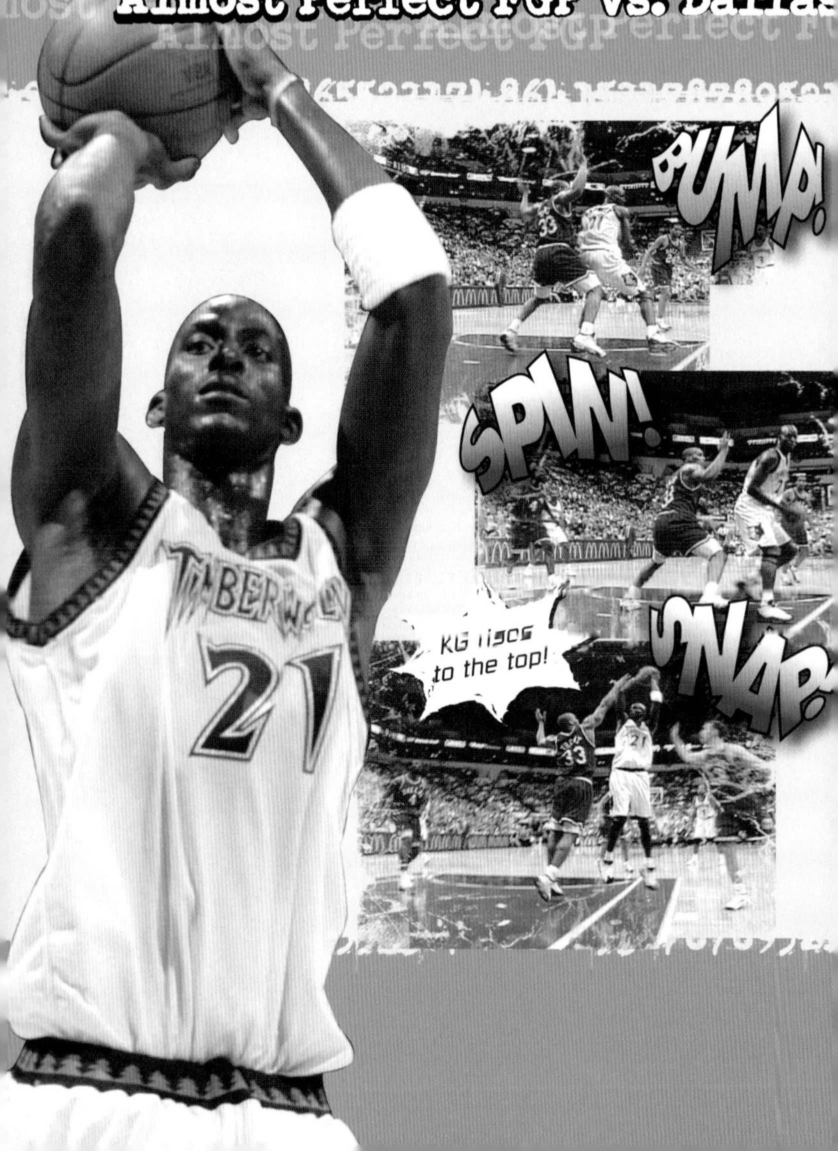
BUMP!
SPIN!
KG rises to the top!
SNAP!

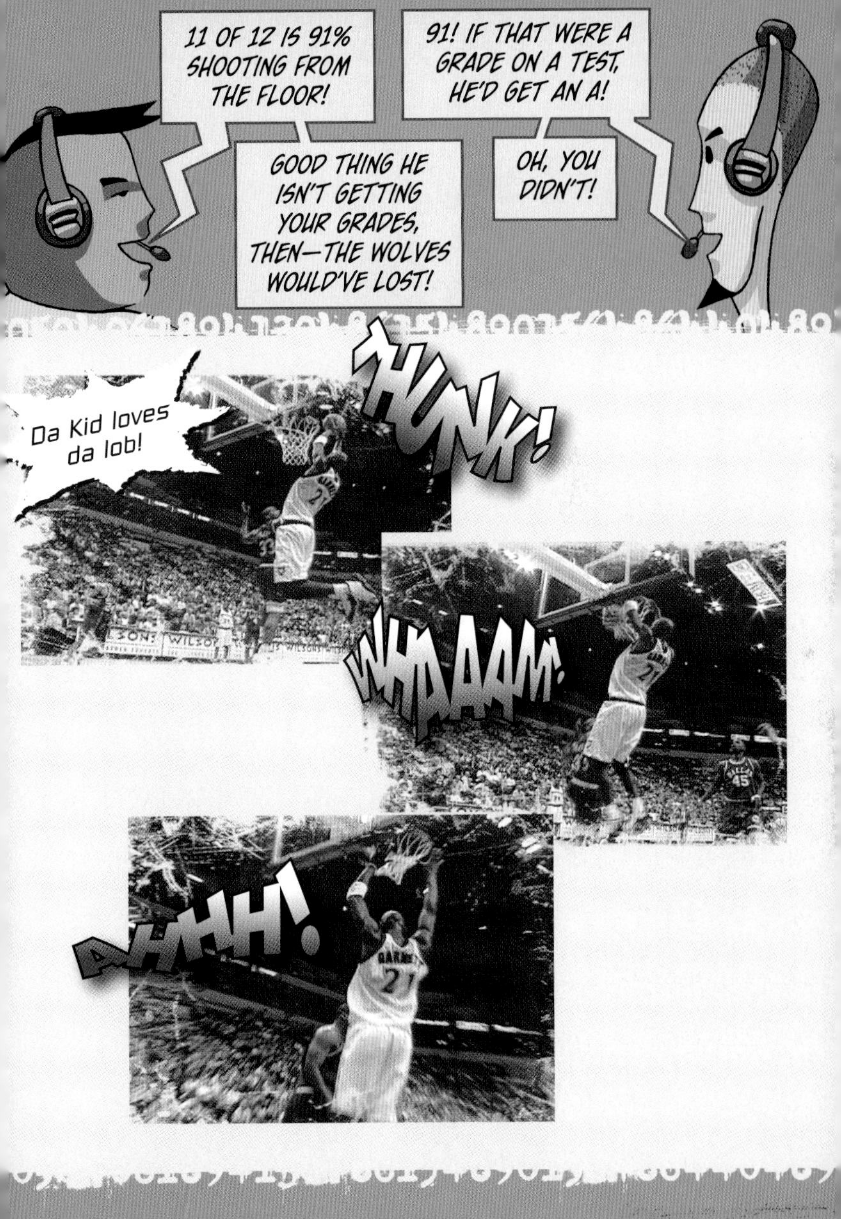
11 OF 12 IS 91% SHOOTING FROM THE FLOOR!
91! IF THAT WERE A GRADE ON A TEST, HE'D GET AN A!
GOOD THING HE ISN'T GETTING YOUR GRADES, THEN—THE WOLVES WOULD'VE LOST!
OH, YOU DIDN'T!
Da Kid loves da lob!
THUNK!
WHAAAM!
AHHH!

March 5, 2003: 24 Rebounds vs. Sacramento!

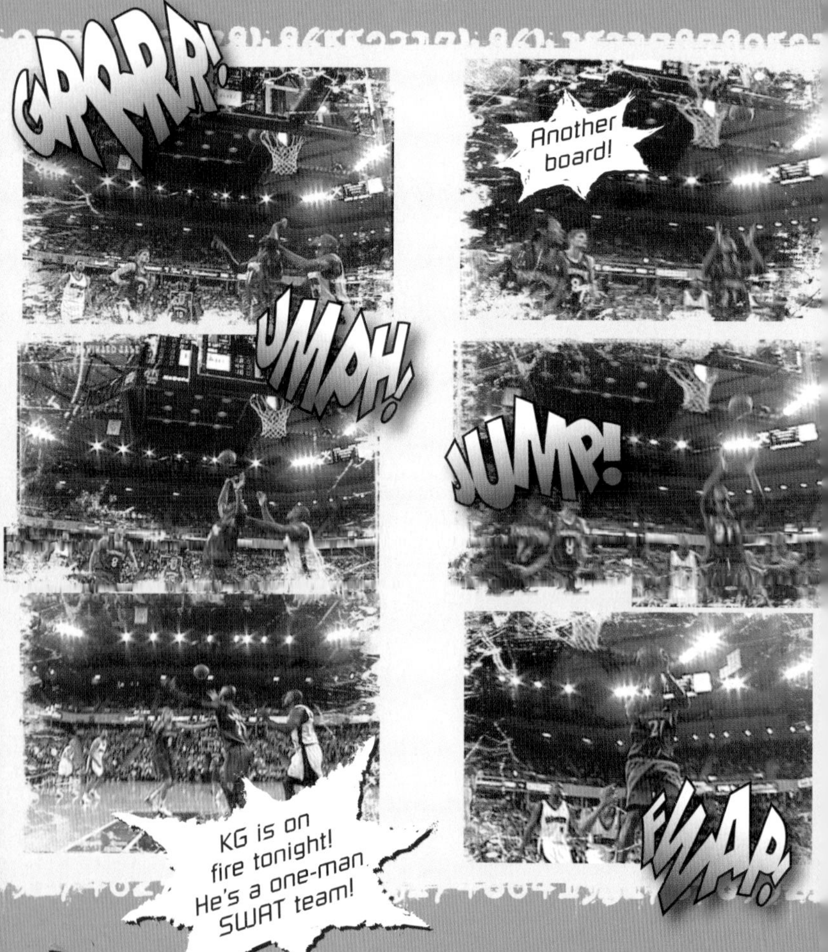
GRRRR!
Another board!
UMPH!
JUMP!
KG is on fire tonight! He's a one-man SWAT team!
FLAP!

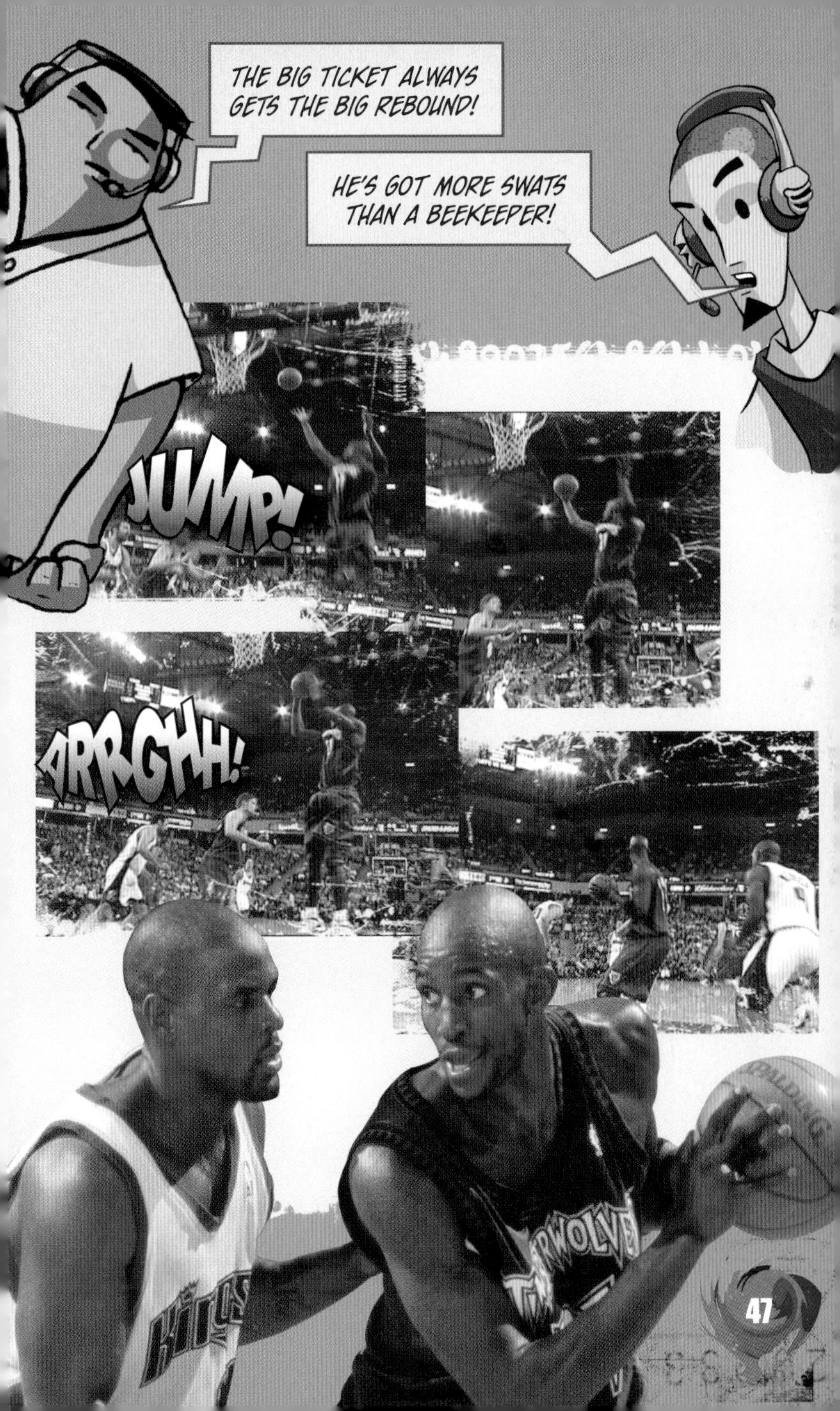

THE BIG TICKET ALWAYS GETS THE BIG REBOUND!
HE'S GOT MORE SWATS THAN A BEEKEEPER!
JUMP!
ARRGHH!

greatest moments

February 16, 2003:
37 Points, 22 Boards vs. Golden State

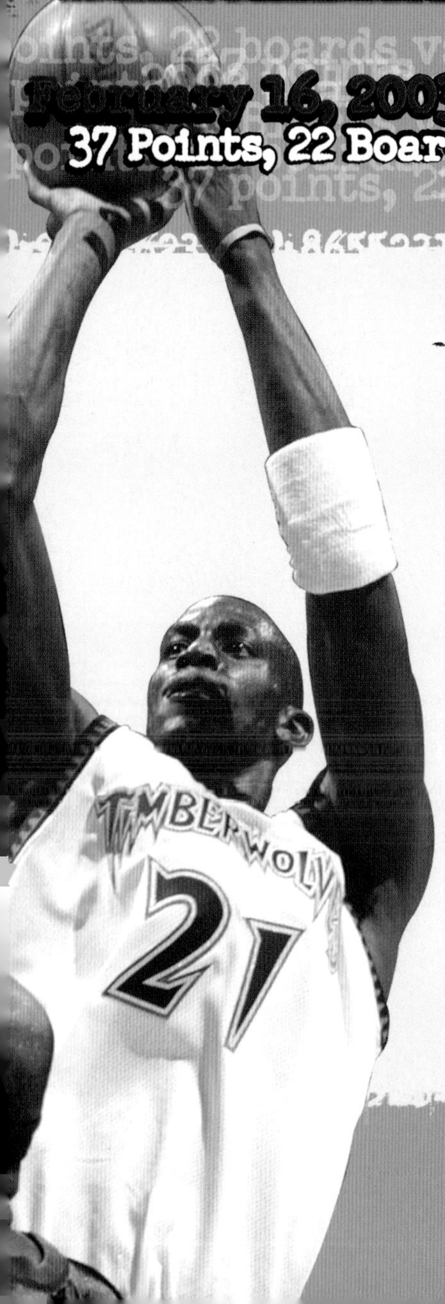

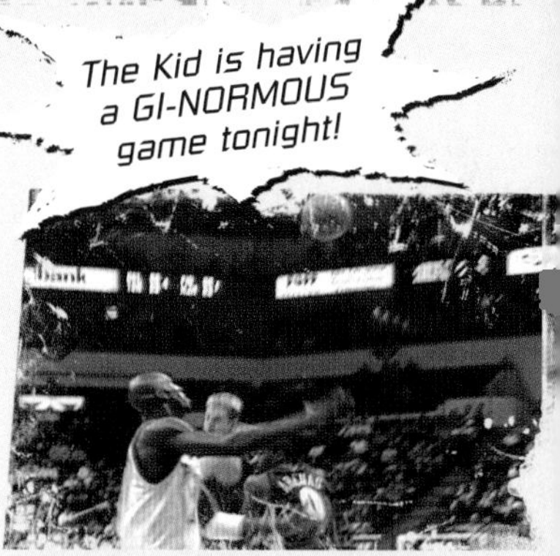
The Kid is having a GI-NORMOUS game tonight!

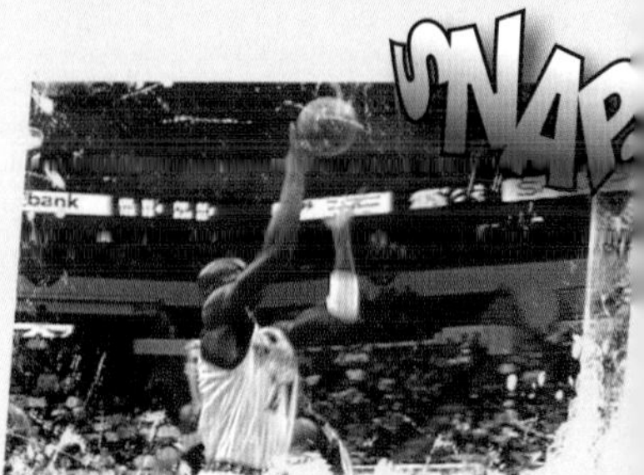
SNAP!

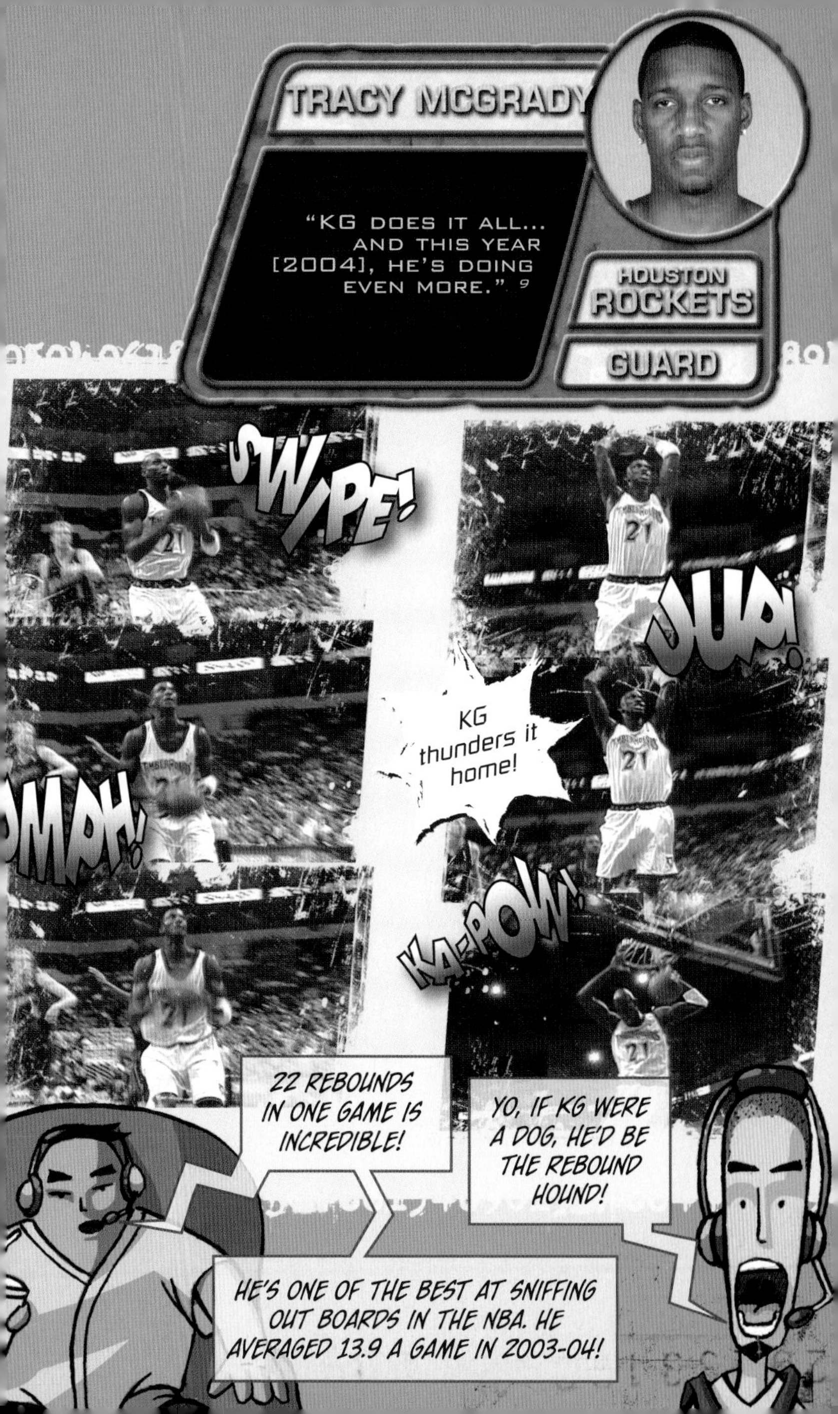
TRACY MCGRADY
"KG DOES IT ALL... AND THIS YEAR [2004], HE'S DOING EVEN MORE." 9
HOUSTON ROCKETS
GUARD
SWIPE!
JUMP!
KG thunders it home!
OMPH!
KA-POW!
22 REBOUNDS IN ONE GAME IS INCREDIBLE!
YO, IF KG WERE A DOG, HE'D BE THE REBOUND HOUND!
HE'S ONE OF THE BEST AT SNIFFING OUT BOARDS IN THE NBA. HE AVERAGED 13.9 A GAME IN 2003-04!

February 16, 2003:
37 Points, 22 Boards vs. Golden State

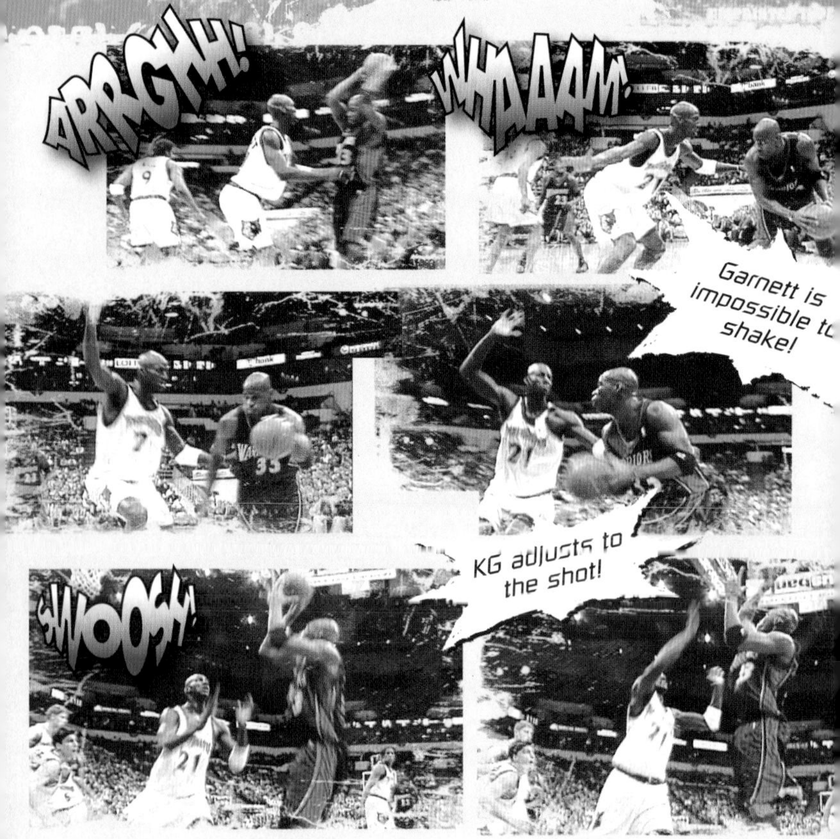
ARRGH!
WHAAAM!
Garnett is impossible to shake!
KG adjusts to the shot!
SWOOSH!

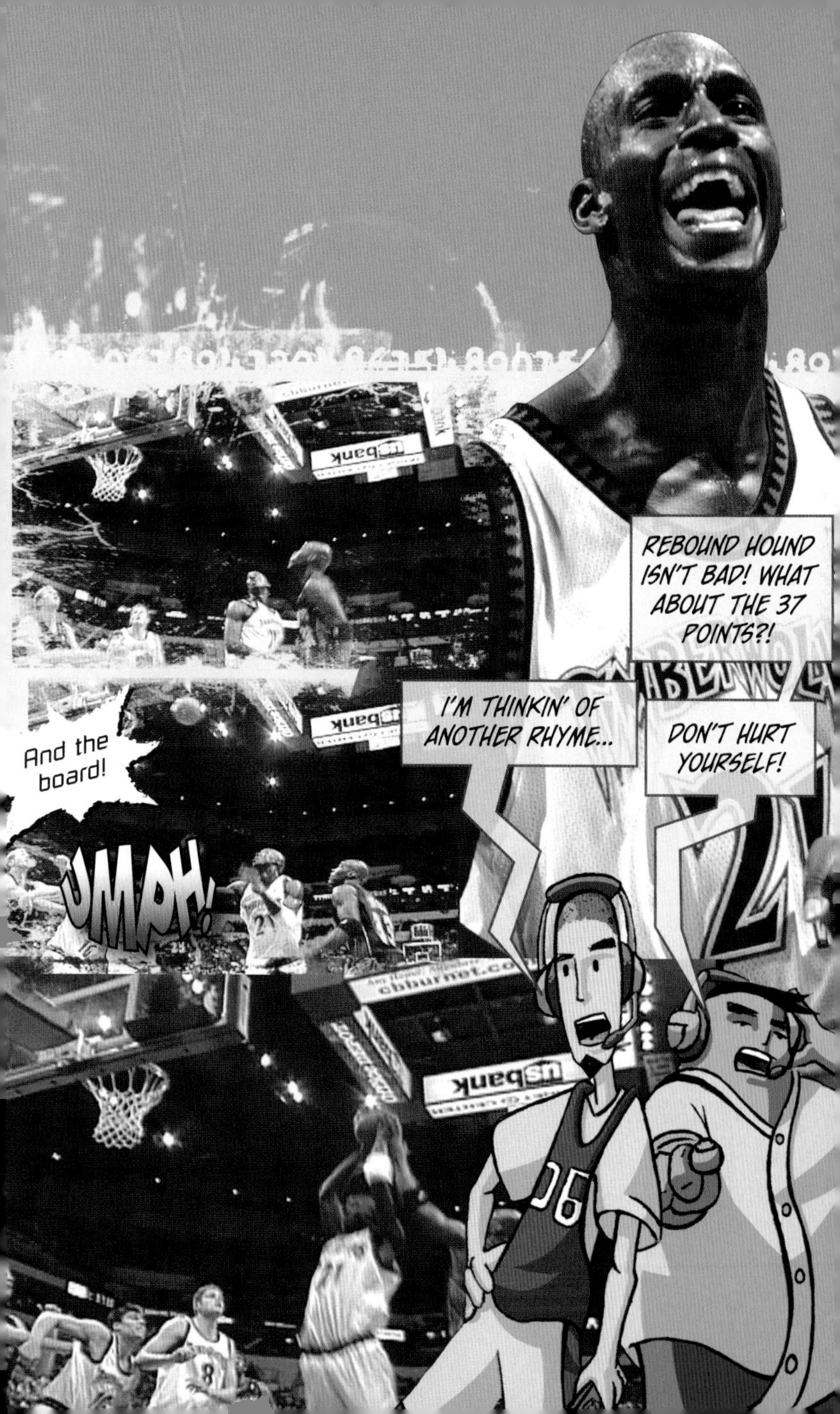
And the board!
UMPH!
REBOUND HOUND ISN'T BAD! WHAT ABOUT THE 37 POINTS?!
I'M THINKIN' OF ANOTHER RHYME...
DON'T HURT YOURSELF!

December 7, 2003: Clippers Buzzer Beater!

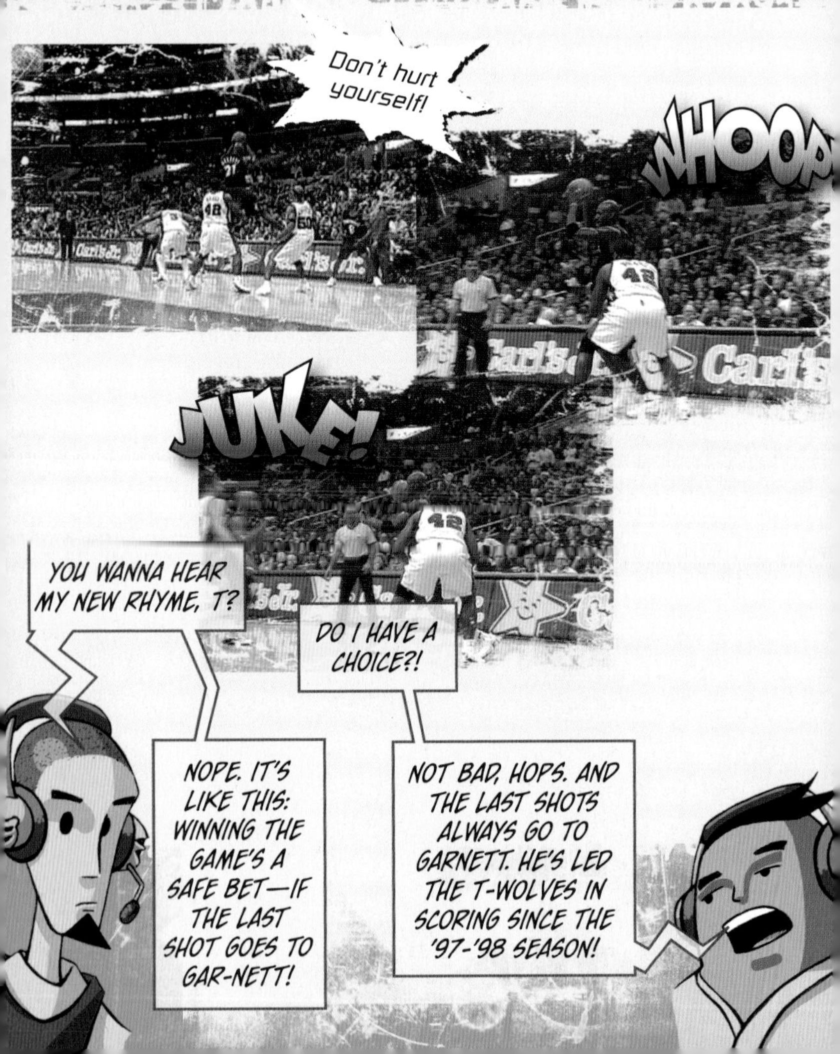
Don't hurt yourself!
WHOOP
JUKE!
YOU WANNA HEAR MY NEW RHYME, T?
DO I HAVE A CHOICE?!
NOPE. IT'S LIKE THIS: WINNING THE GAME'S A SAFE BET—IF THE LAST SHOT GOES TO GAR-NETT!
NOT BAD, HOPS. AND THE LAST SHOTS ALWAYS GO TO GARNETT. HE'S LED THE T-WOLVES IN SCORING SINCE THE '97-'98 SEASON!

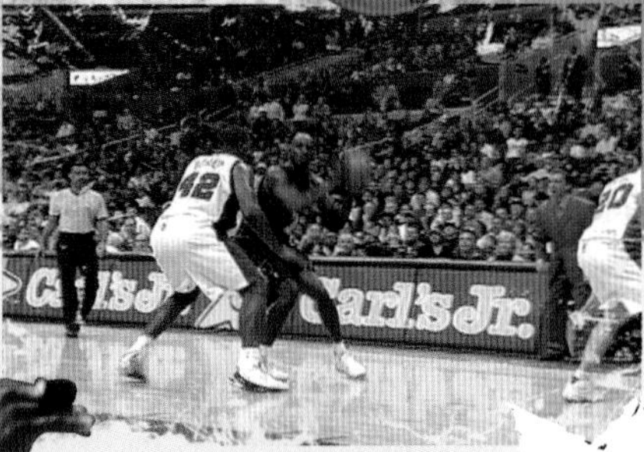

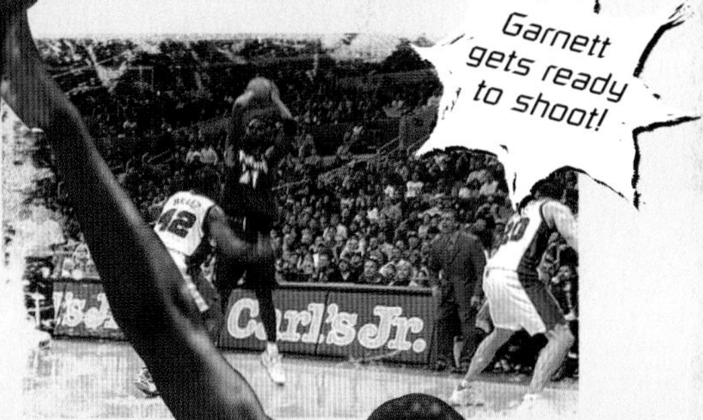
Garnett gets ready to shoot!

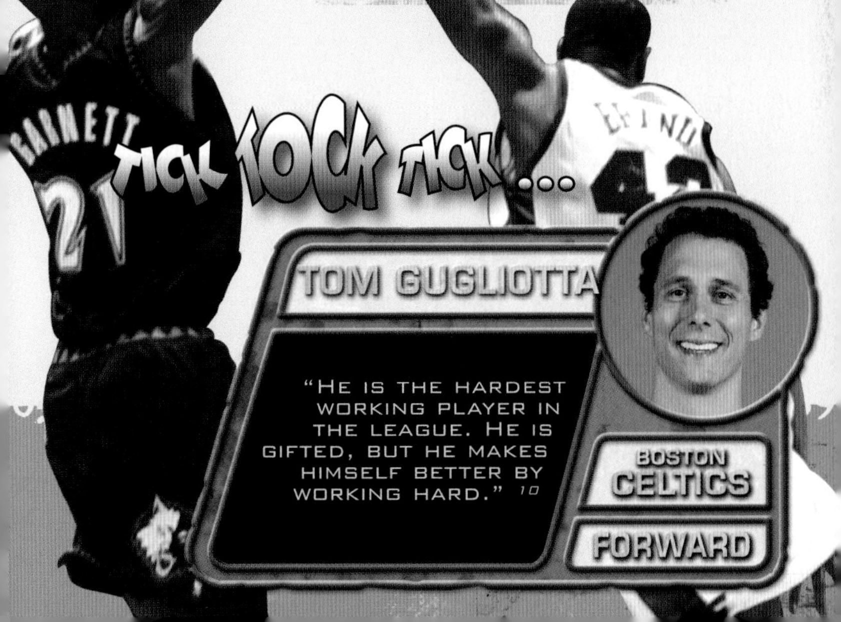
GARNETT
21
TICK TOCK TICK...

TOM GUGLIOTTA

"He is the hardest working player in the league. He is gifted, but he makes himself better by working hard." [10]

BOSTON CELTICS

FORWARD

greatest moments

December 5, 2003: Two Threes with 30 Seconds Left in Sacramento!

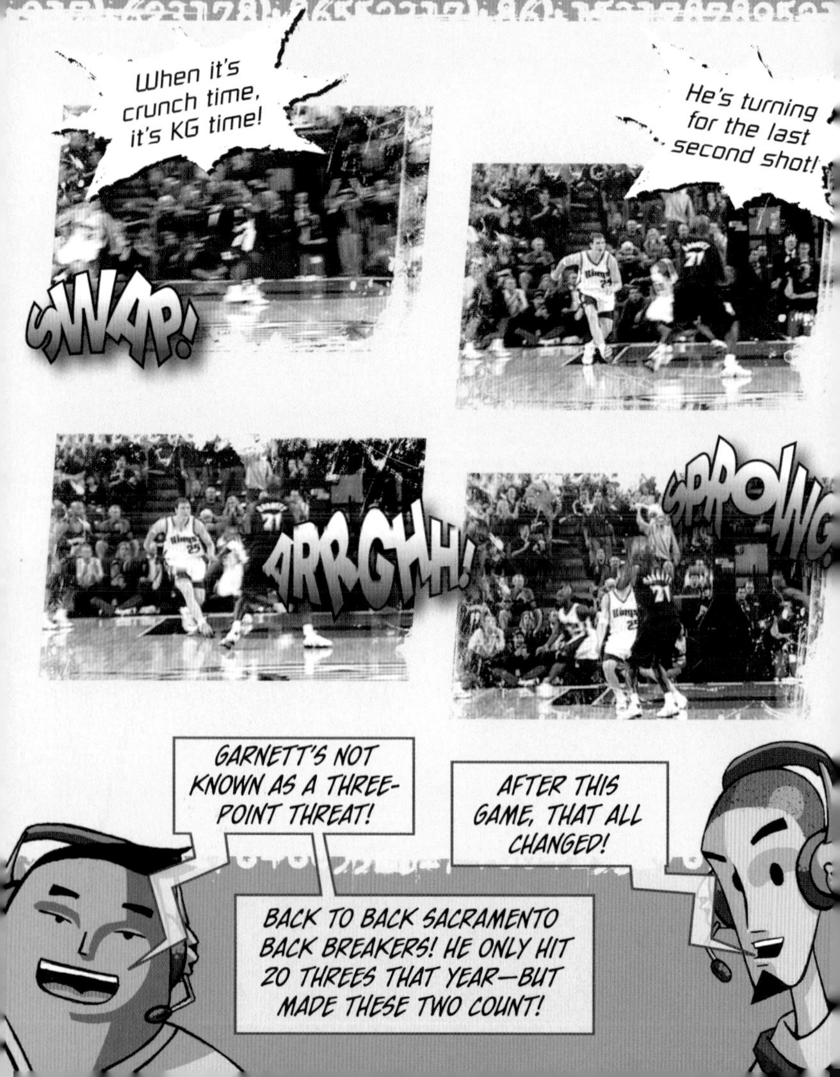

When it's crunch time, it's KG time!
SWAP!
He's turning for the last second shot!
ARRGHH!
SPROING!
GARNETT'S NOT KNOWN AS A THREE-POINT THREAT!
AFTER THIS GAME, THAT ALL CHANGED!
BACK TO BACK SACRAMENTO BACK BREAKERS! HE ONLY HIT 20 THREES THAT YEAR—BUT MADE THESE TWO COUNT!

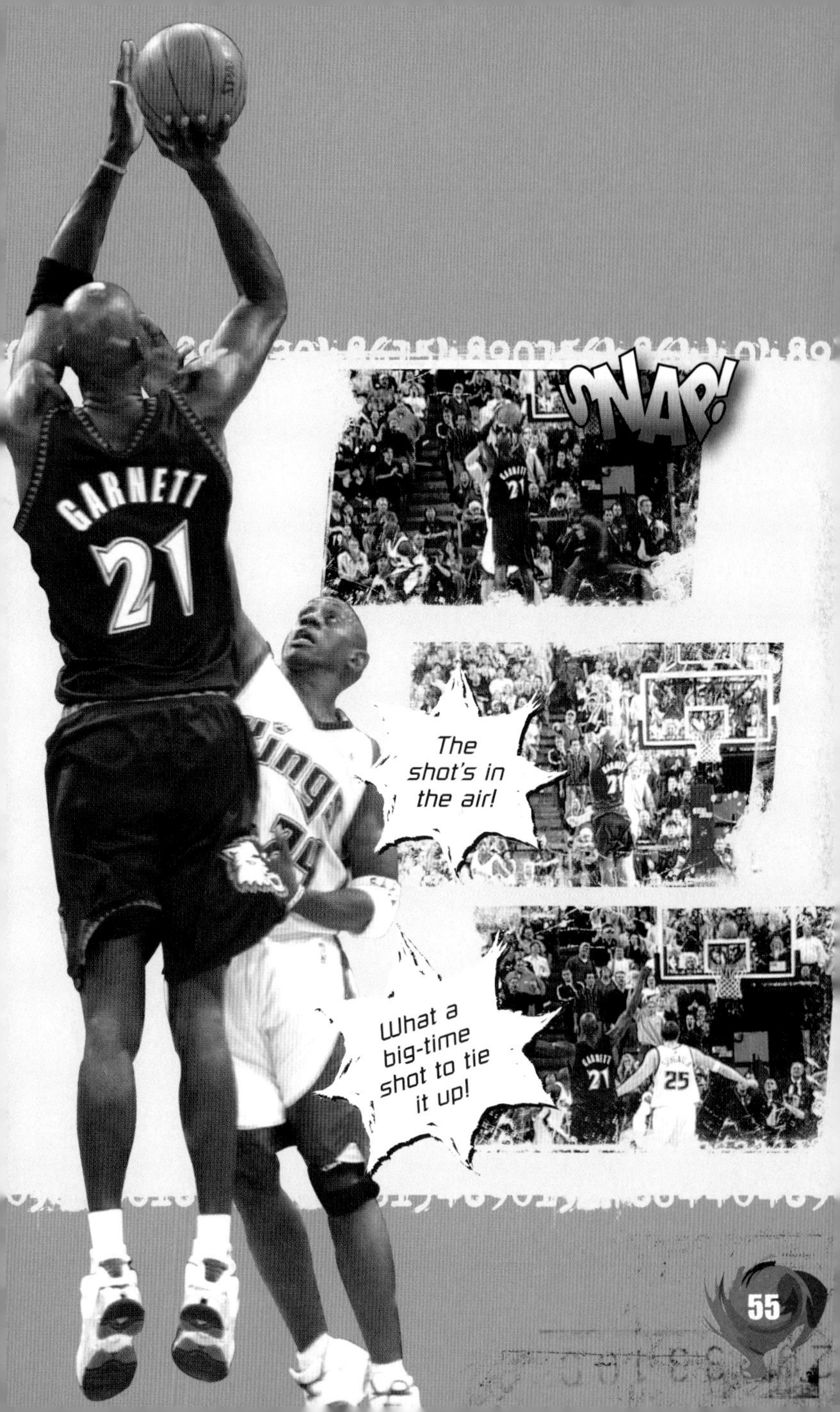
SNAP!
The shot's in the air!
What a big-time shot to tie it up!

December 5, 2003: Two Threes with 30 Seconds Left in Sacramento!

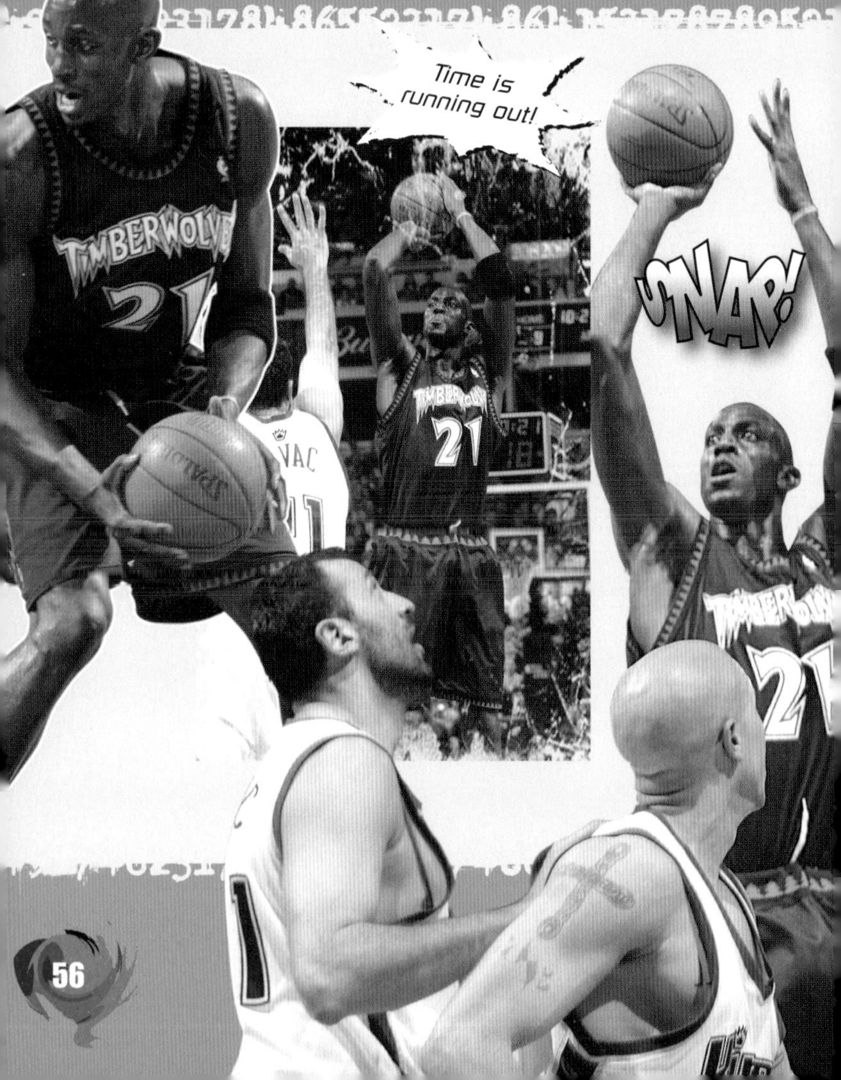
Time is running out!
SNAP!

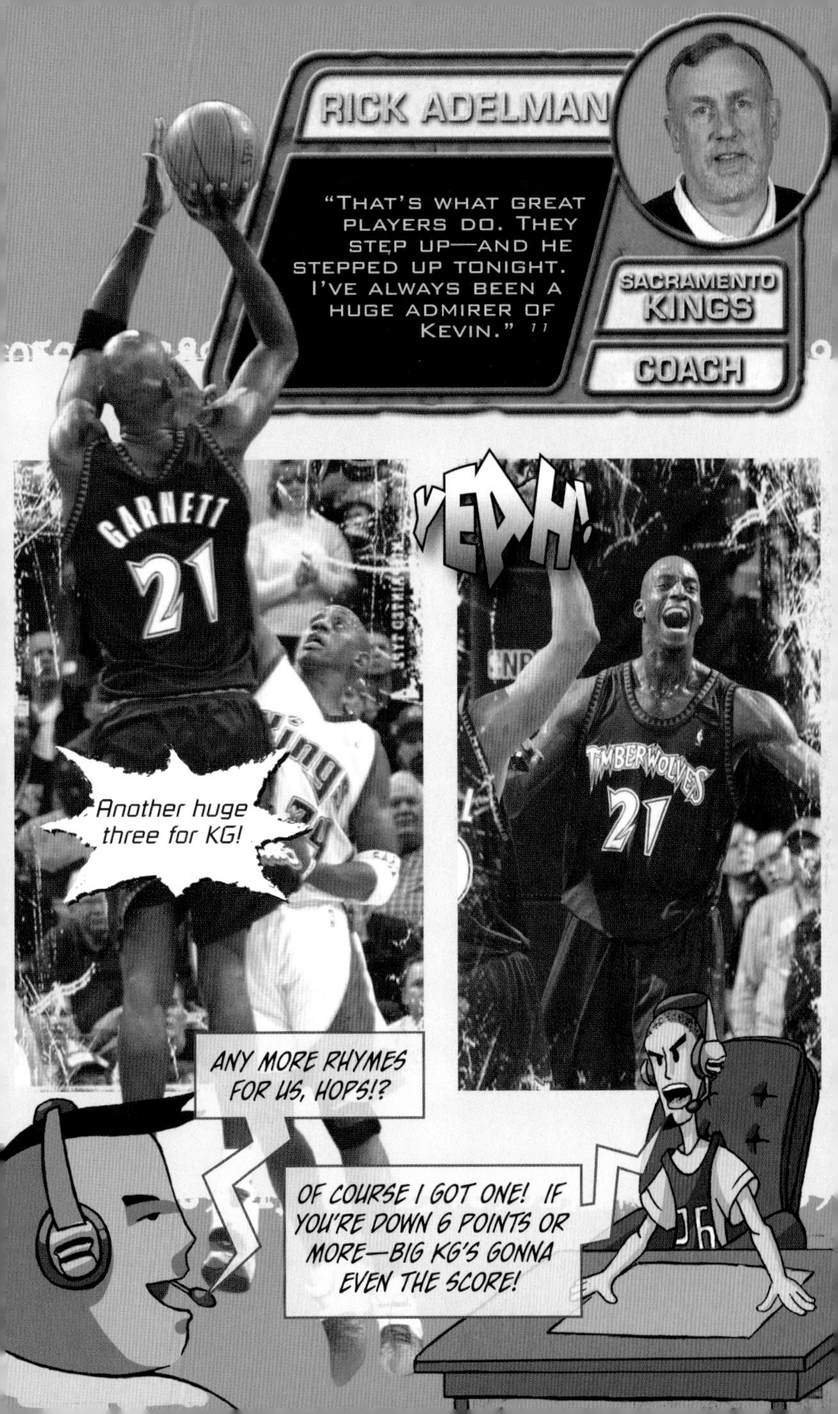

RICK ADELMAN
"THAT'S WHAT GREAT PLAYERS DO. THEY STEP UP—AND HE STEPPED UP TONIGHT. I'VE ALWAYS BEEN A HUGE ADMIRER OF KEVIN." 11
SACRAMENTO KINGS
COACH
GARNETT 21
YEAH!
TIMBERWOLVES 21
Another huge three for KG!
ANY MORE RHYMES FOR US, HOPS!?
OF COURSE I GOT ONE! IF YOU'RE DOWN 6 POINTS OR MORE—BIG KG'S GONNA EVEN THE SCORE!

March 9, 2003: Triple-Double and Career High Assists vs. Phoenix

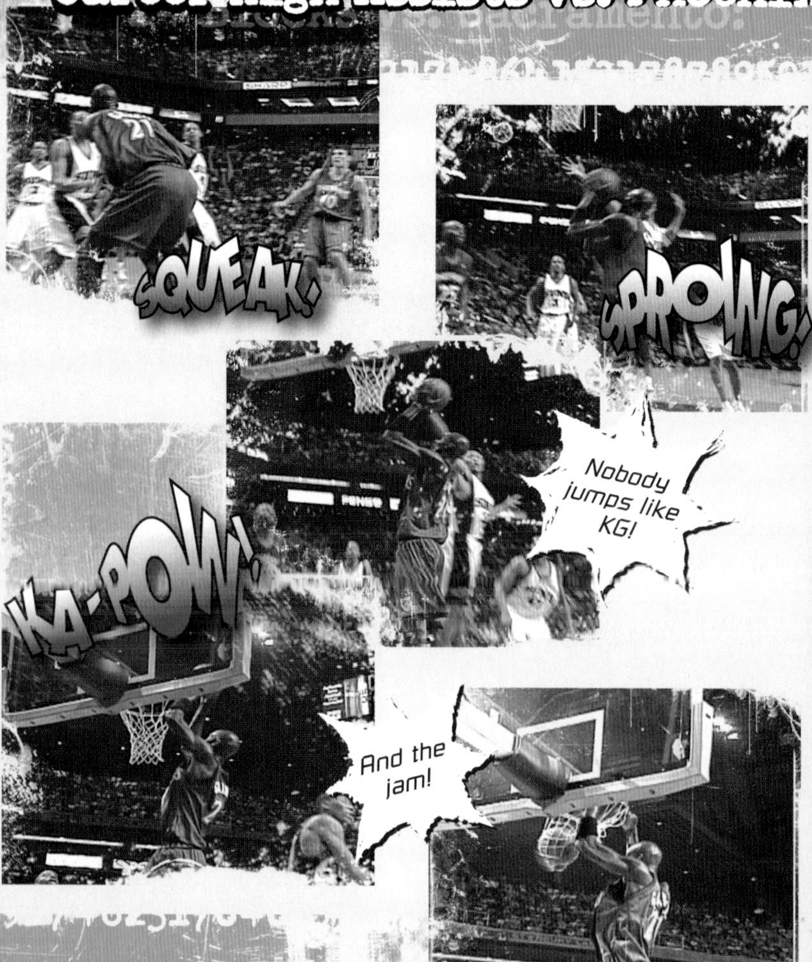
SQUEAK!
SPROING!
KA-POW!
Nobody jumps like KG!
And the jam!

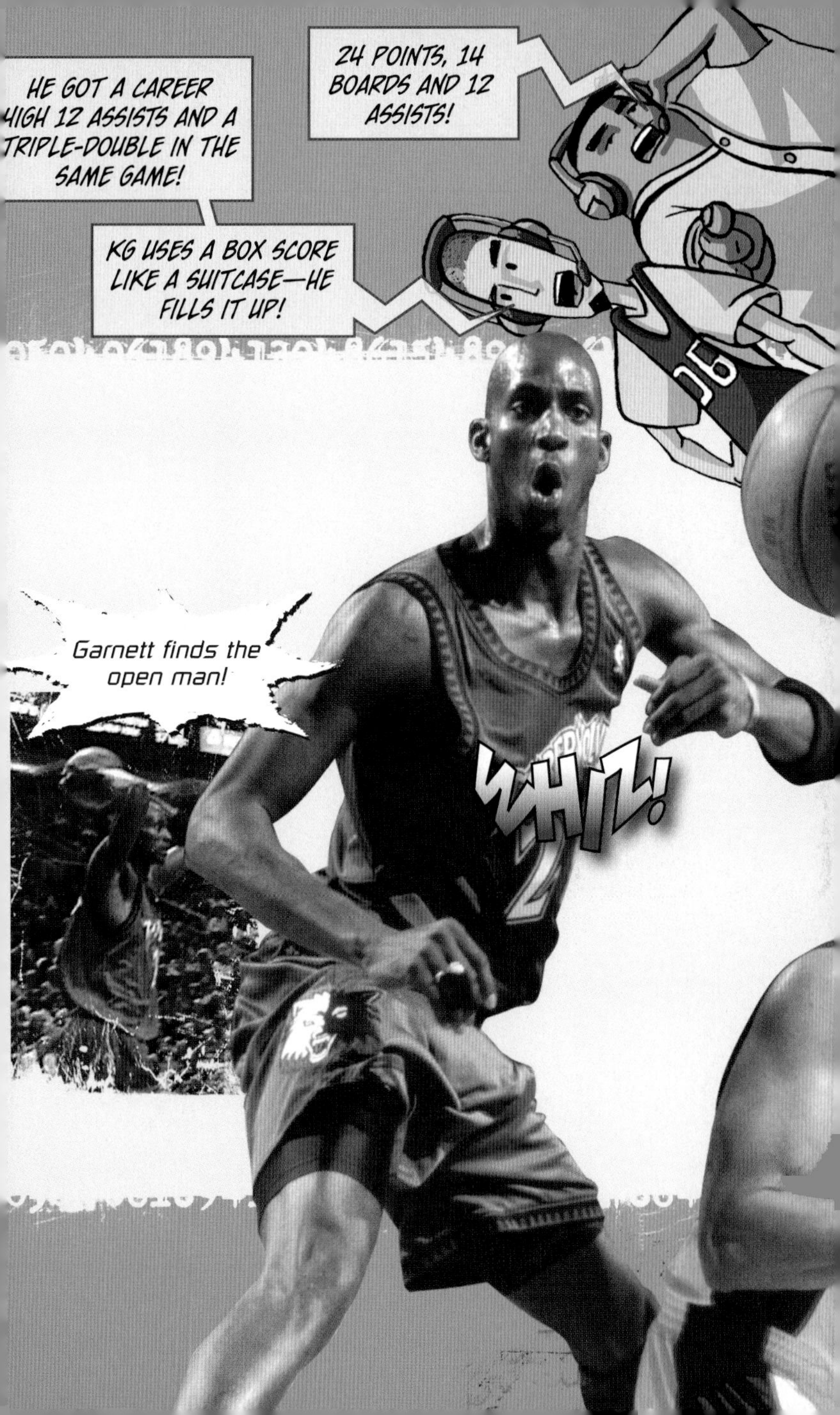
24 POINTS, 14 BOARDS AND 12 ASSISTS!
HE GOT A CAREER HIGH 12 ASSISTS AND A TRIPLE-DOUBLE IN THE SAME GAME!
KG USES A BOX SCORE LIKE A SUITCASE—HE FILLS IT UP!
Garnett finds the open man!
WHIZ!

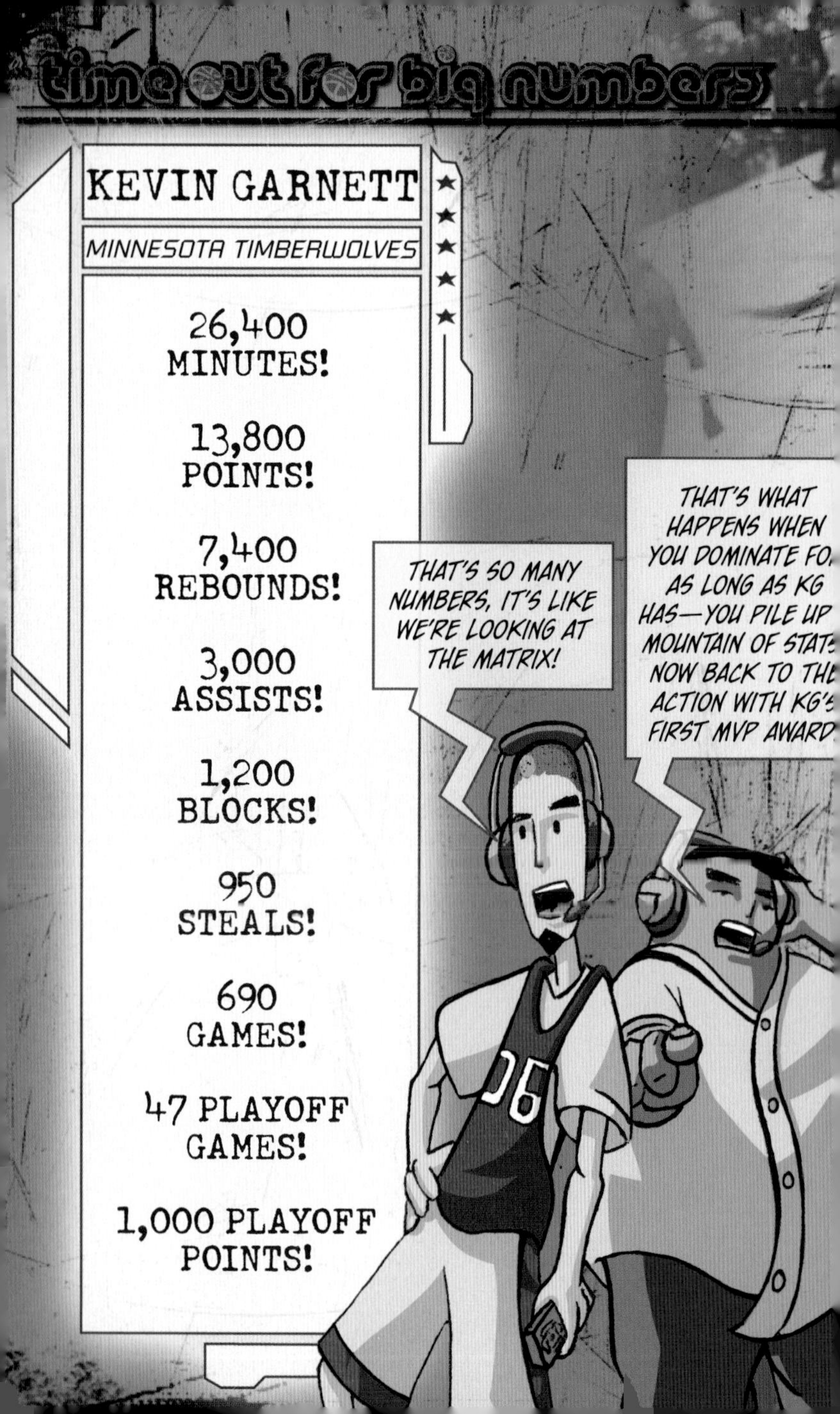
time out for big numbers
KEVIN GARNETT
MINNESOTA TIMBERWOLVES
26,400 MINUTES!
13,800 POINTS!
7,400 REBOUNDS!
3,000 ASSISTS!
1,200 BLOCKS!
950 STEALS!
690 GAMES!
47 PLAYOFF GAMES!
1,000 PLAYOFF POINTS!
THAT'S SO MANY NUMBERS, IT'S LIKE WE'RE LOOKING AT THE MATRIX!
THAT'S WHAT HAPPENS WHEN YOU DOMINATE FO AS LONG AS KG HAS—YOU PILE UP MOUNTAIN OF STAT NOW BACK TO TH ACTION WITH KG' FIRST MVP AWARD
06

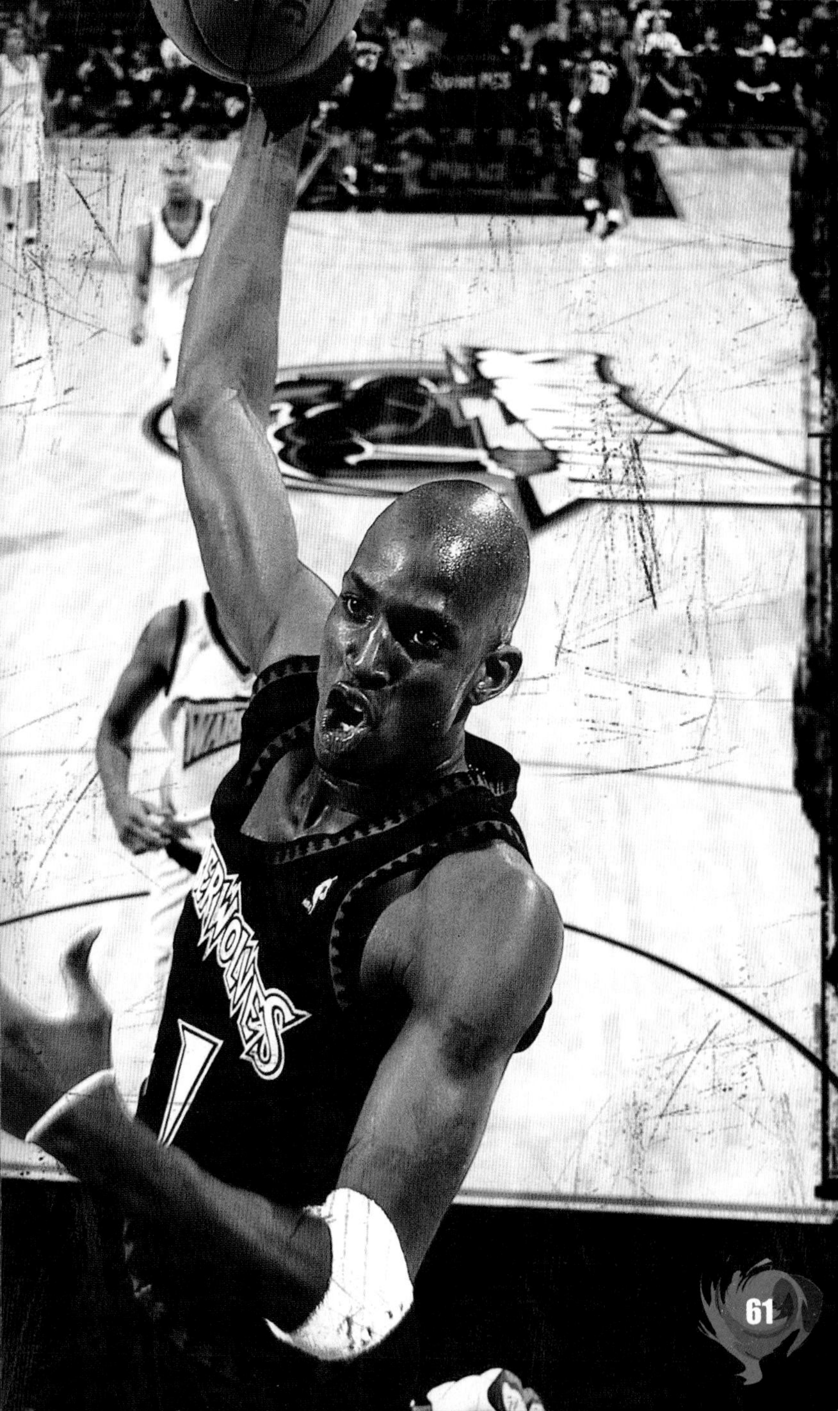

greatest moments

May 3, 2004:
Named 2003-04 NBA MVP!

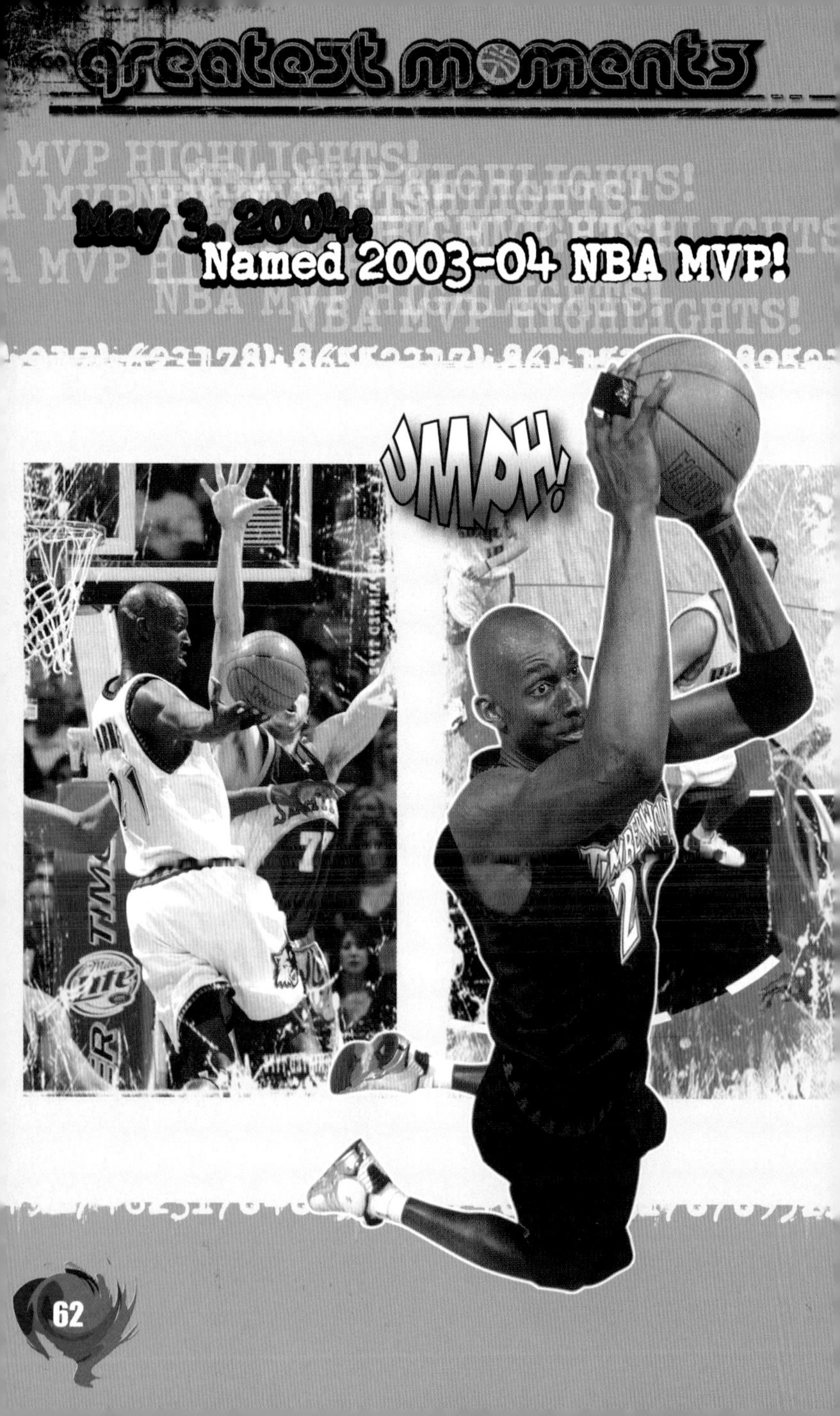
UMPH!

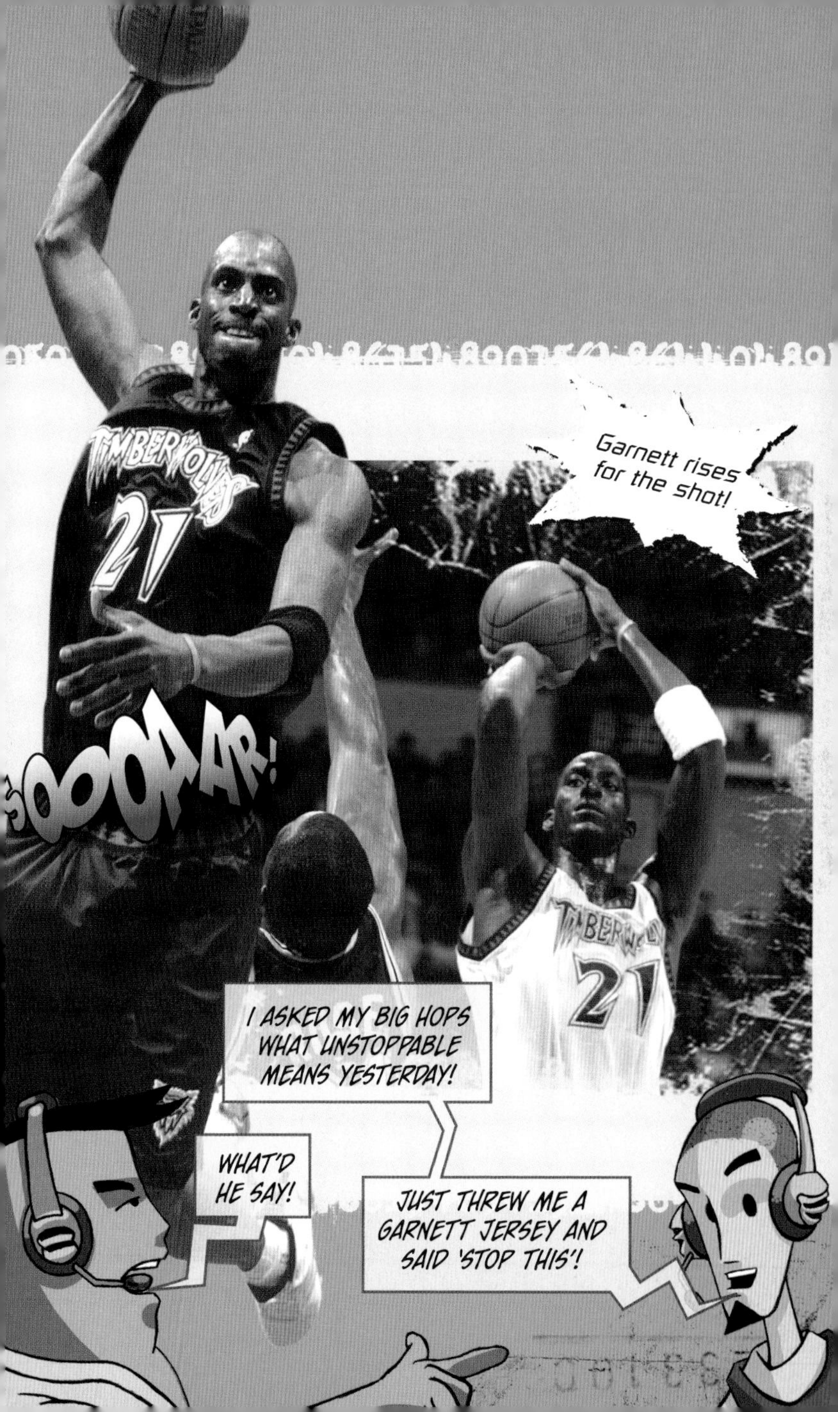
Garnett rises for the shot!
SOOOAR!
I ASKED MY BIG HOPS WHAT UNSTOPPABLE MEANS YESTERDAY!
WHAT'D HE SAY!
JUST THREW ME A GARNETT JERSEY AND SAID 'STOP THIS'!

greatest moments

May 3, 2004: Named 2003-04 NBA MVP!

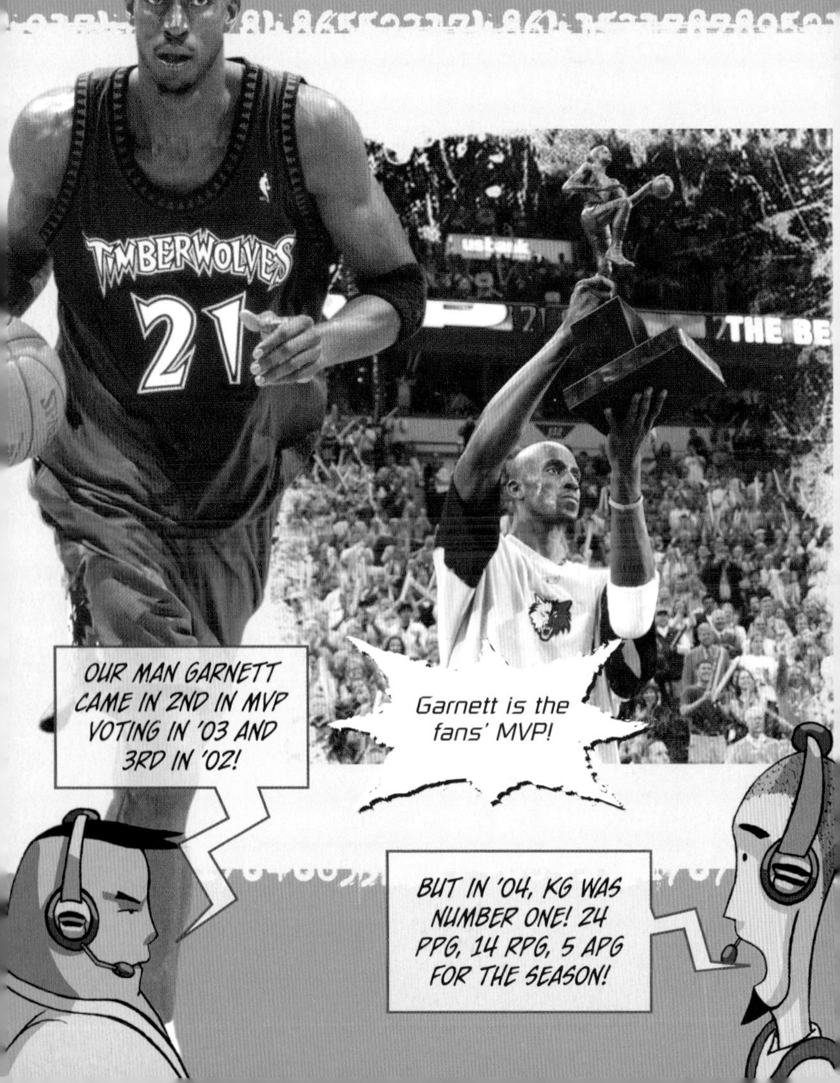

TRACY MCGRADY

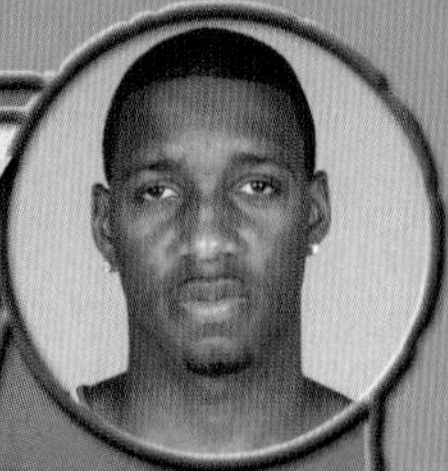

"DEFENSIVELY, HE'S PHENOMENAL. OFFENSIVELY, HE'S GETTING HIS TEAMMATES INVOLVED. I'VE GOT A LOT OF RESPECT FOR HIM AS A PLAYER AND A PERSON." [12]

HOUSTON ROCKETS

GUARD

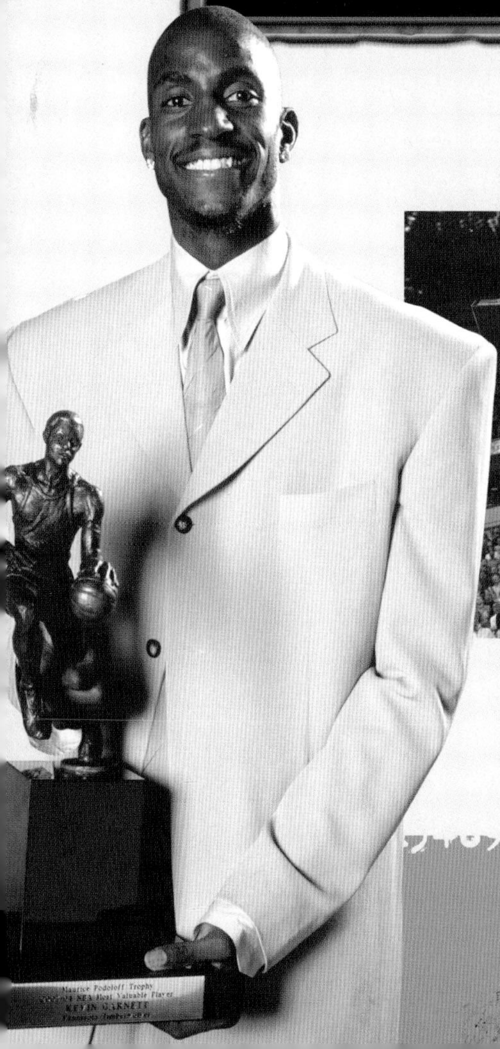
Maurice Podoloff Trophy
KEVIN GARNETT

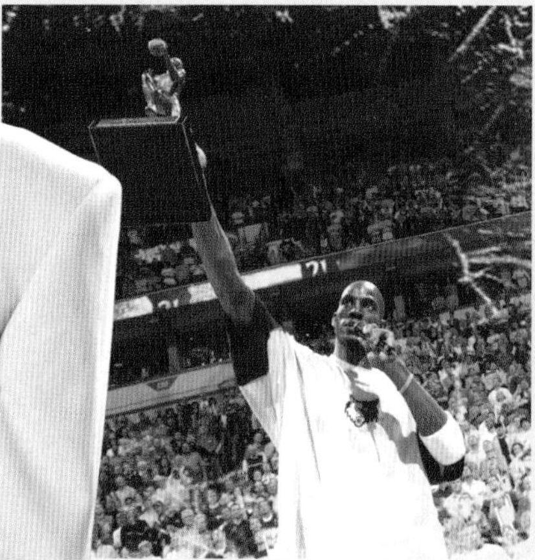

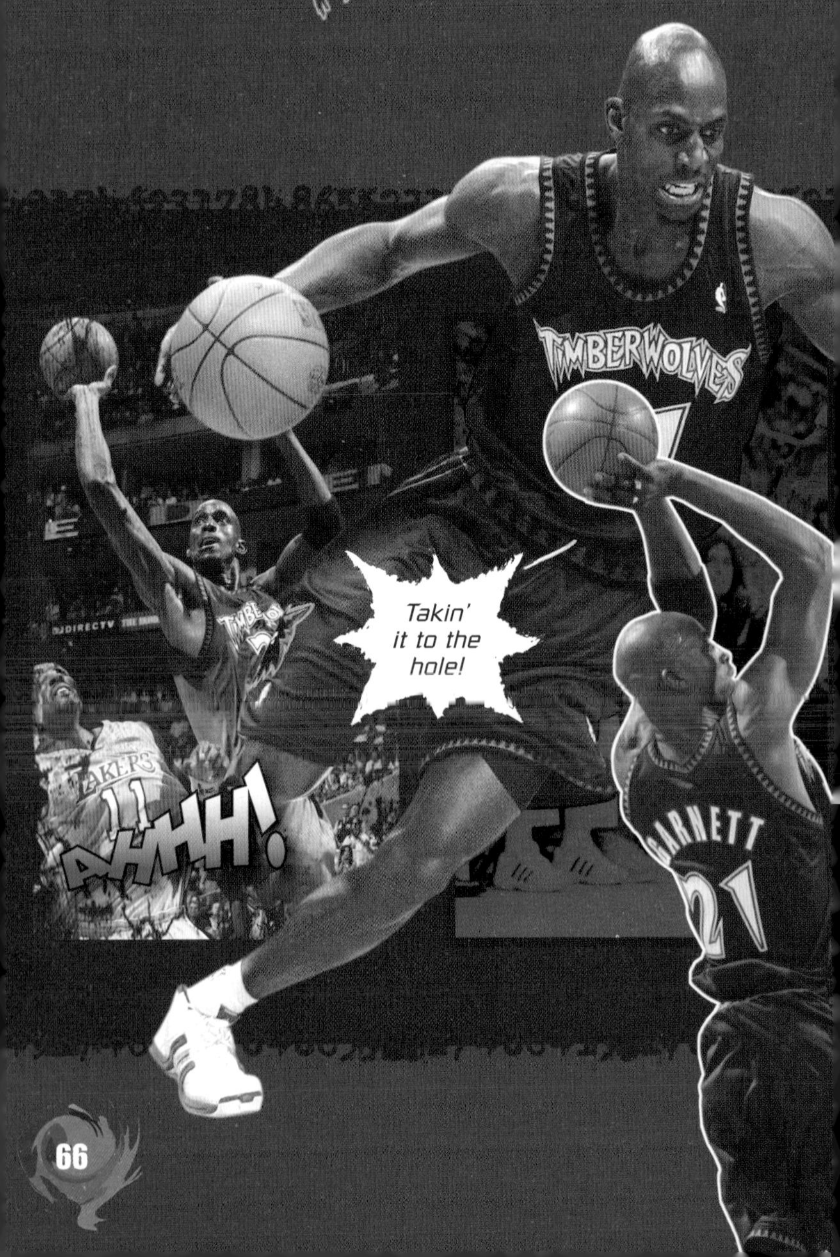
Takin' it to the hole!
AHHH!

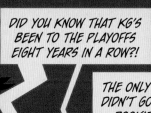

DID YOU KNOW THAT KG'S BEEN TO THE PLAYOFFS EIGHT YEARS IN A ROW?!

THE ONLY YEAR HE DIDN'T GO WAS HIS ROOKIE YEAR!

IT'S ONLY FAIR—HE HAD TO GIVE THE LEAGUE A YEAR TO GET READY!

KG won't be denied his first playoff series win!

April 30, 2004:
Knocking out Denver the in First Round

Knocking out Denver
ing out Denver
in First Round
ocking out Denver
in First Round
in First Round

The Big Ticket makes a big move!

ZOOM

KG's gonna dunk—no matter who's in his way!

GRRRR!

30 AND 20 IN BACK-TO-BACK GAMES!

BIG NUMBERS FROM A BIG TICKET! AND HIS FIRST PLAYOFF SERIES WIN!

SPROING!

KG KNEW IT WAS A MAKE—OR—BREAK SERIES FOR THE WOLVES, SO HE MADE IT HIS MISSION TO WIN.

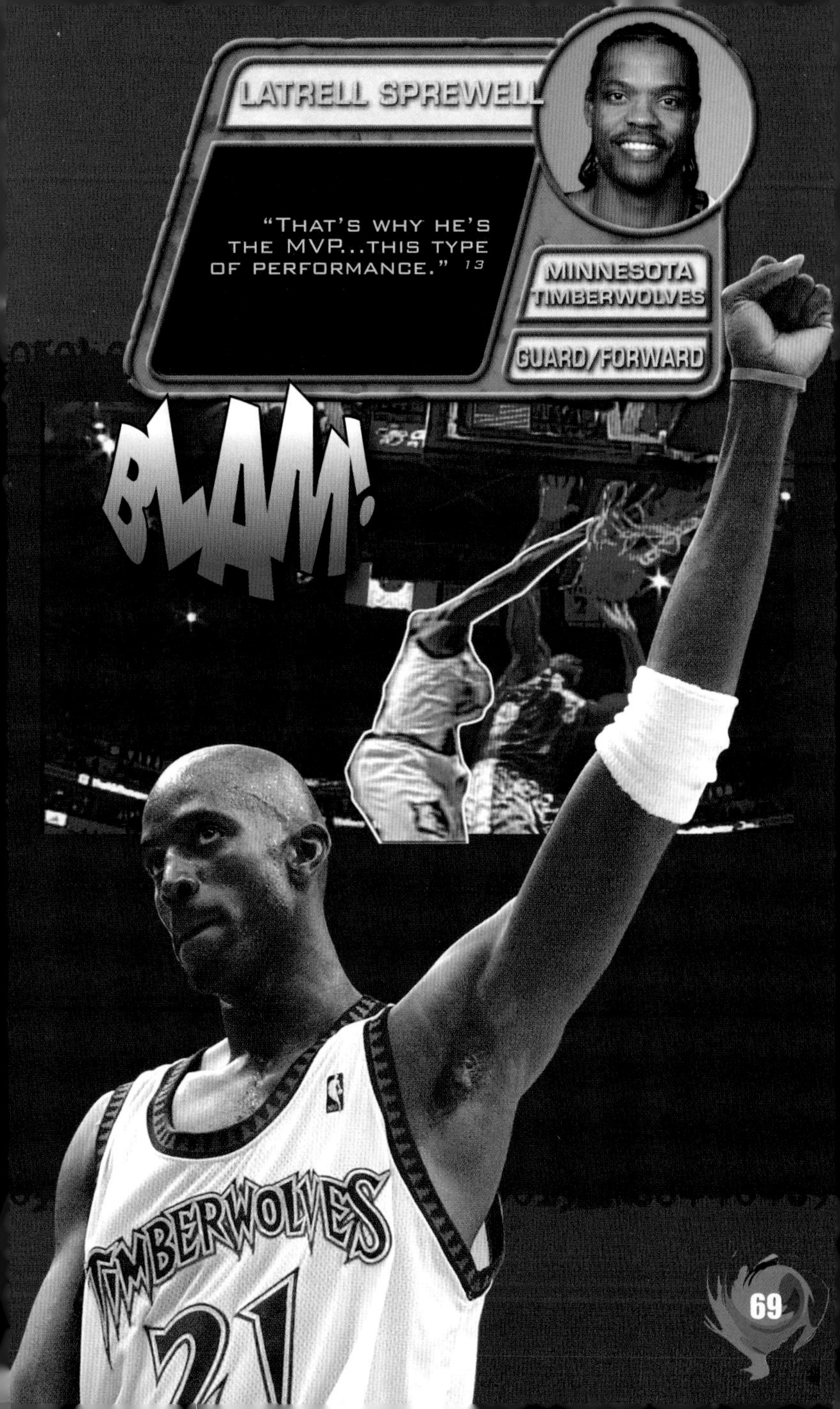
LATRELL SPREWELL
"THAT'S WHY HE'S THE MVP...THIS TYPE OF PERFORMANCE." 13
MINNESOTA TIMBERWOLVES
GUARD/FORWARD
BLAM!
TIMBERWOLVES
21

April 22, 2003: Monster Playoff Game vs. Lakers

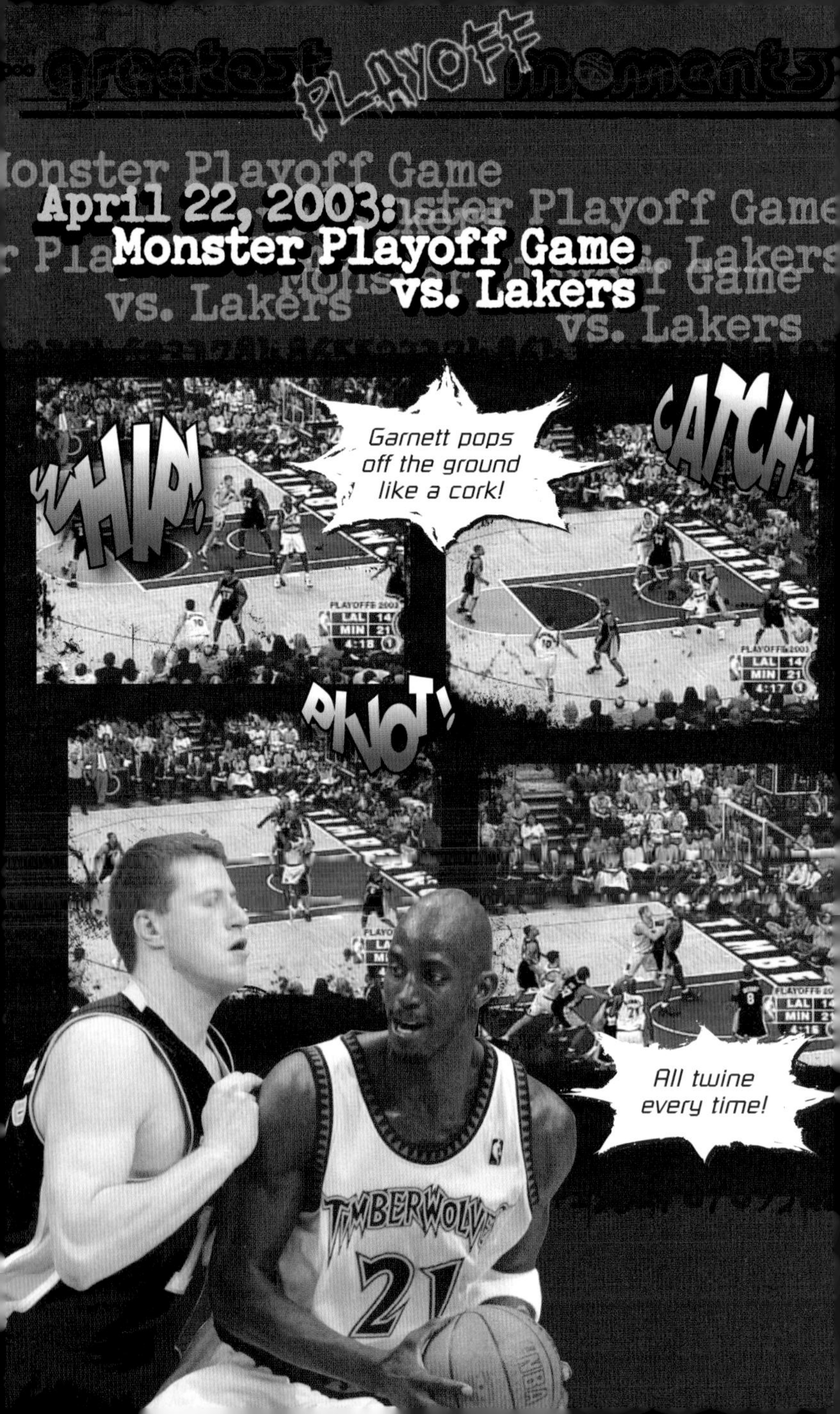
WHIP!
Garnett pops off the ground like a cork!
CATCH!
PIVOT!
All twine every time!

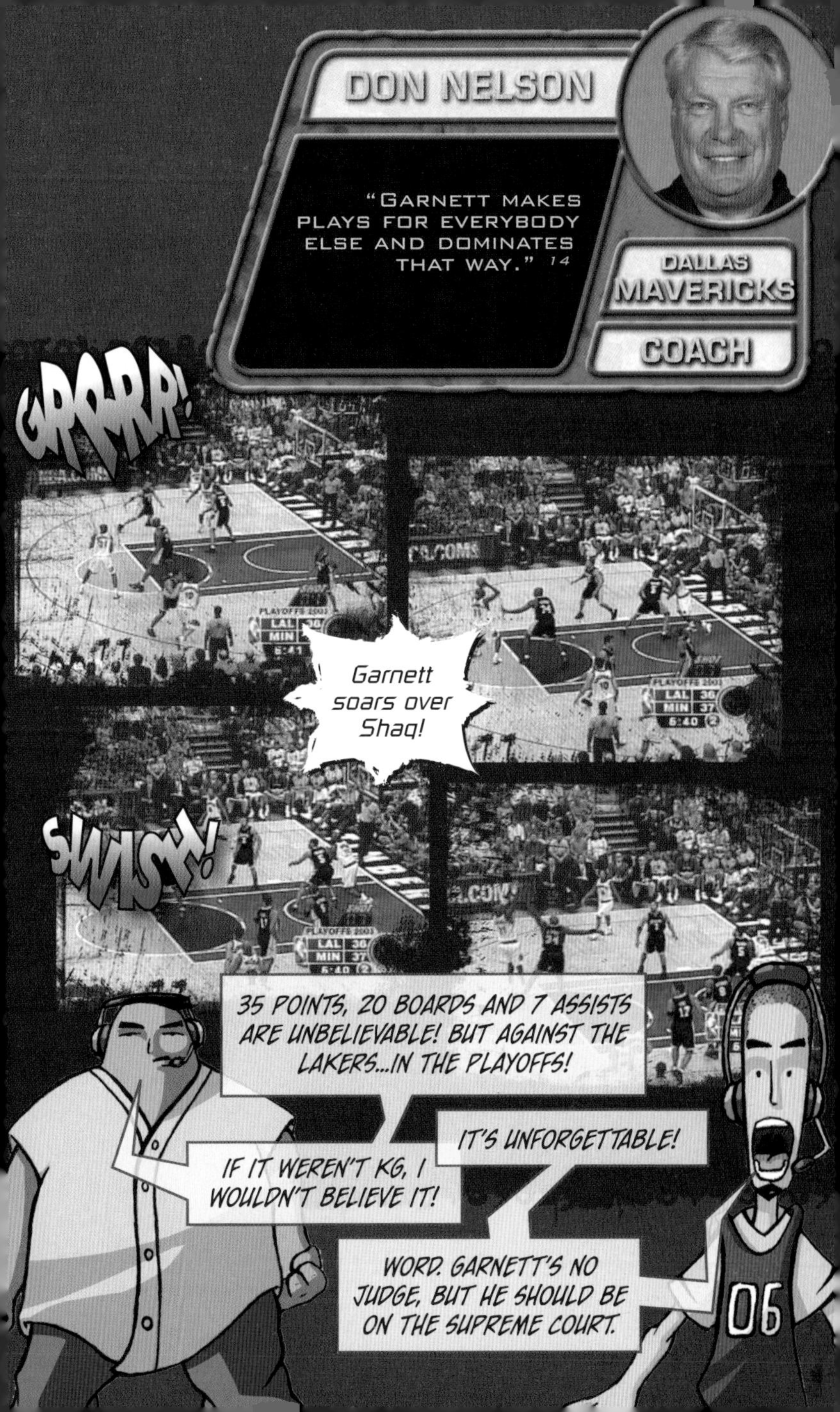
DON NELSON
"GARNETT MAKES PLAYS FOR EVERYBODY ELSE AND DOMINATES THAT WAY." 14
DALLAS MAVERICKS
COACH
Garnett soars over Shaq!
SWISH!
35 POINTS, 20 BOARDS AND 7 ASSISTS ARE UNBELIEVABLE! BUT AGAINST THE LAKERS...IN THE PLAYOFFS!
IF IT WEREN'T KG, I WOULDN'T BELIEVE IT!
IT'S UNFORGETTABLE!
WORD. GARNETT'S NO JUDGE, BUT HE SHOULD BE ON THE SUPREME COURT.

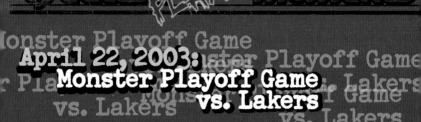

April 22, 2003: Monster Playoff Game vs. Lakers

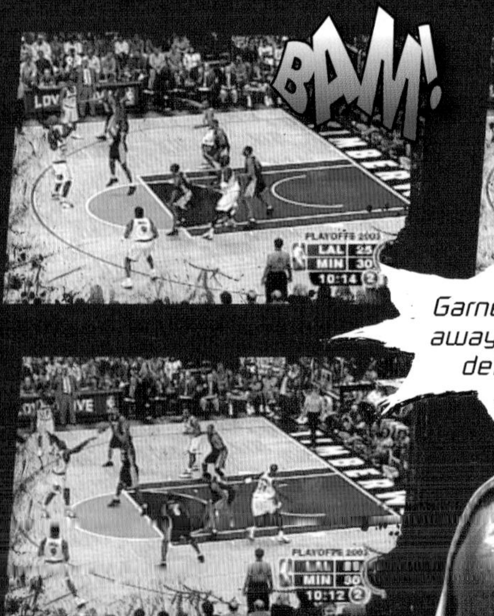
BAM!
PLAYOFFS 2003
LAL 25
MIN 30
10:14 2
Garnett whirls away from his defender!

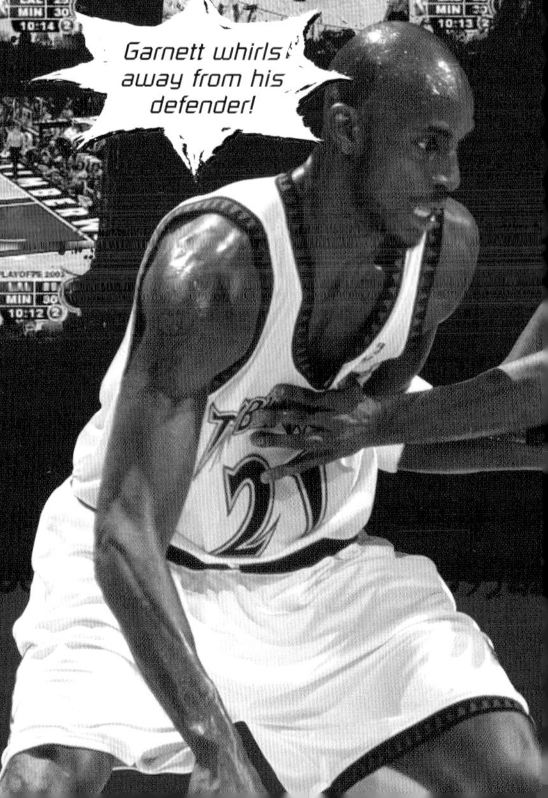

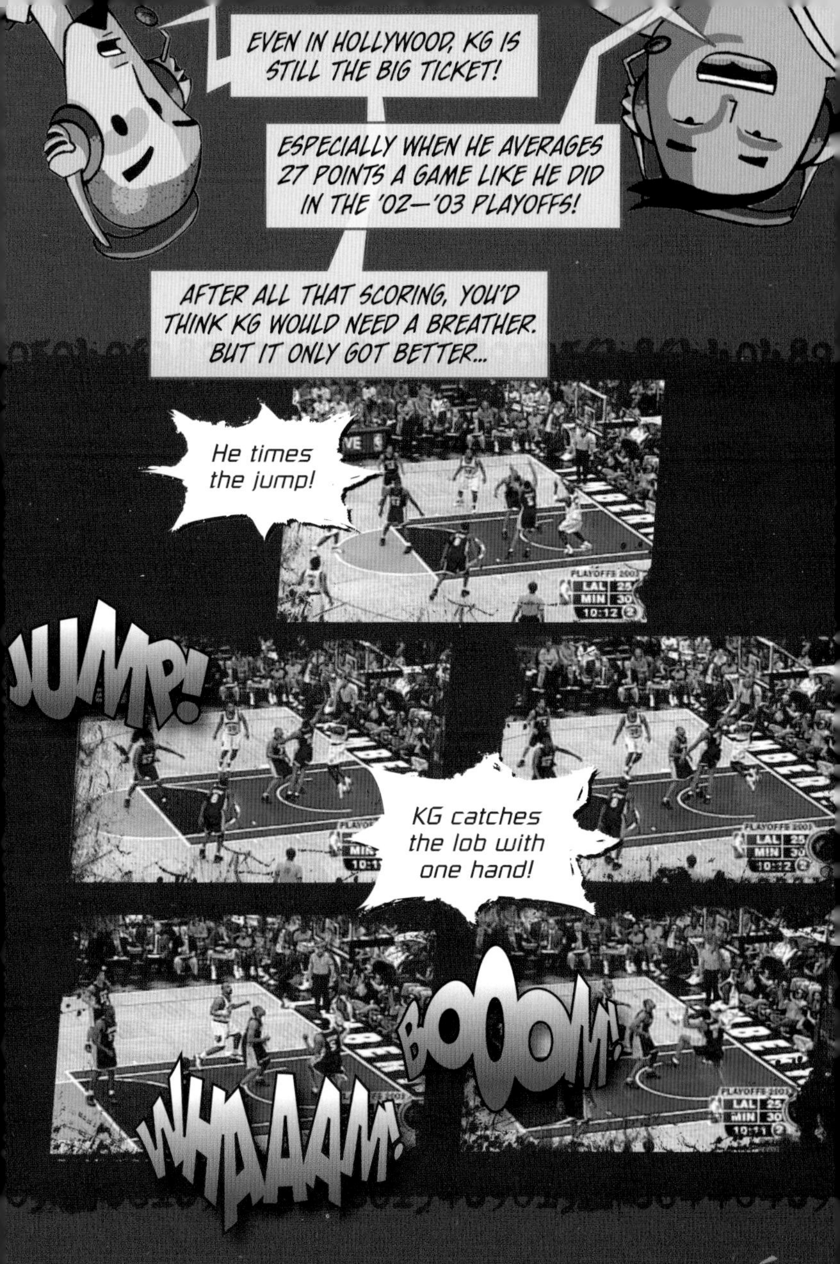
EVEN IN HOLLYWOOD, KG IS STILL THE BIG TICKET!
ESPECIALLY WHEN HE AVERAGES 27 POINTS A GAME LIKE HE DID IN THE '02—'03 PLAYOFFS!
AFTER ALL THAT SCORING, YOU'D THINK KG WOULD NEED A BREATHER. BUT IT ONLY GOT BETTER...
He times the jump!
JUMP!
KG catches the lob with one hand!
WHAAAM!
BOOOM!

May 19, 2004: Garnett Beats Sacramento in Game 7!

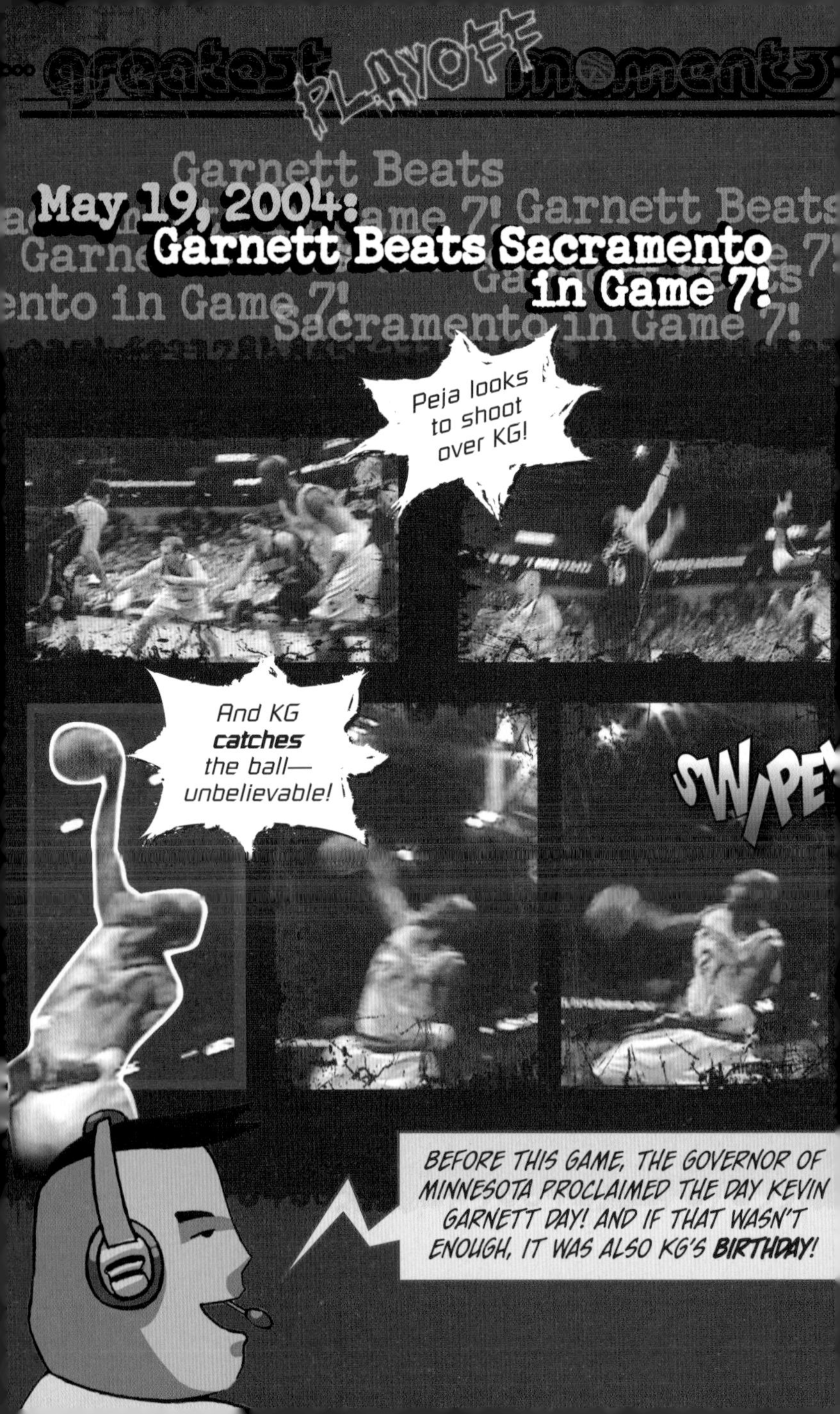
Peja looks to shoot over KG!
And KG **catches** the ball—unbelievable!
SWIPE
BEFORE THIS GAME, THE GOVERNOR OF MINNESOTA PROCLAIMED THE DAY KEVIN GARNETT DAY! AND IF THAT WASN'T ENOUGH, IT WAS ALSO KG'S **BIRTHDAY**!

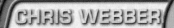

CHRIS WEBBER

"KG IS PROBABLY MY FAVORITE PLAYER IN THE LEAGUE. I LOVE GOING AGAINST HIM." 15

SACRAMENTO KINGS

FORWARD

OUNCE!

See ya!

Another swat!

ARRGHH!

NONE OF THAT PRESSURE BOTHERED MY MAN GARNETT!

SOMETIMES IT TAKES THE BIGGEST STAGE TO HAVE YOUR GREATEST PERFORMANCE! 32 POINTS AND 21 BOARDS IS WHAT I CALL GREAT! BUT IT WAS GARNETT'S FOURTH QUARTER, ON THE NEXT PAGE, THAT WAS LEGENDARY!

May 19, 2004: 13 Straight 4th Quarter Points vs. Sacramento!

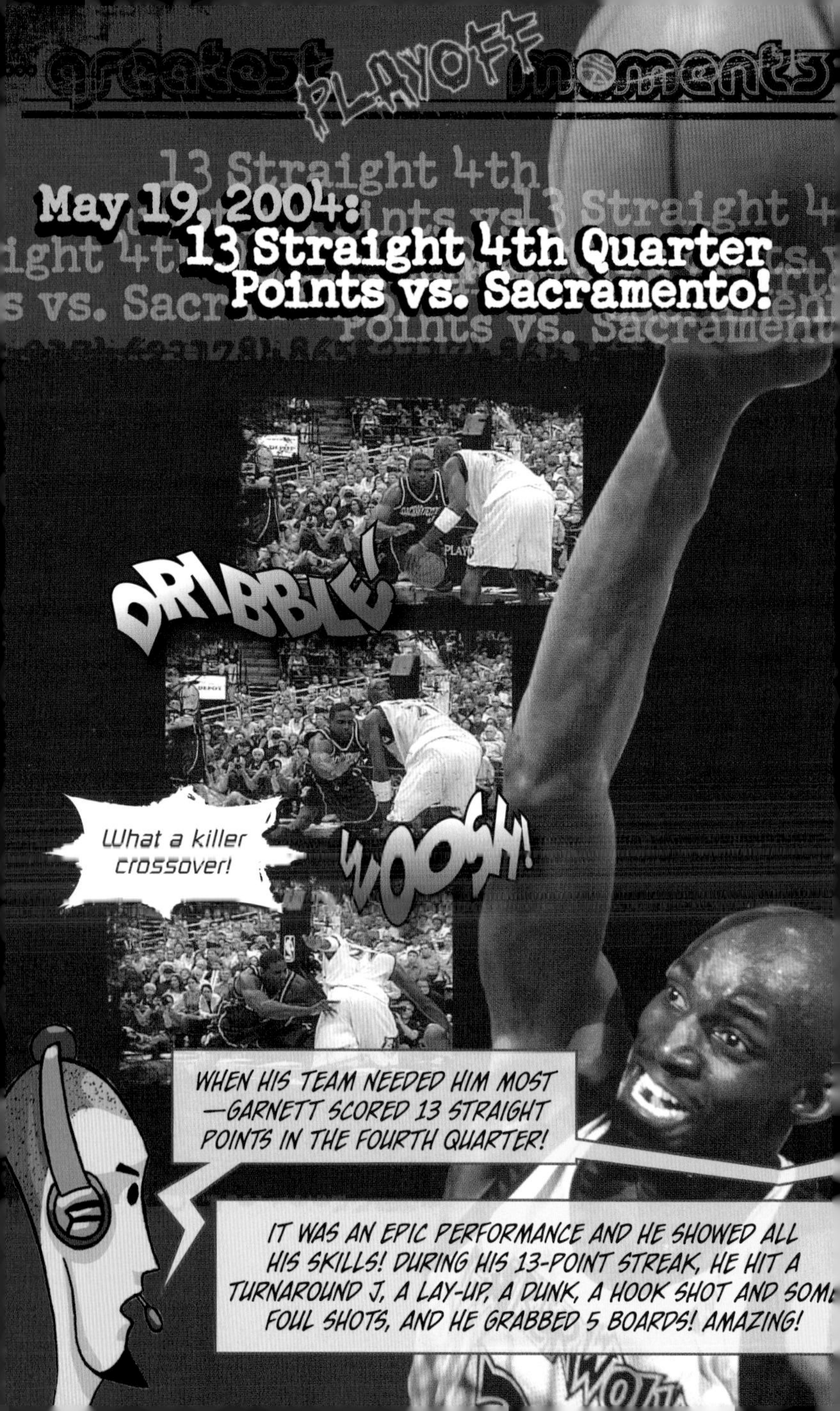
DRIBBLE!
What a killer crossover!
WOOSH!
WHEN HIS TEAM NEEDED HIM MOST—GARNETT SCORED 13 STRAIGHT POINTS IN THE FOURTH QUARTER!
IT WAS AN EPIC PERFORMANCE AND HE SHOWED ALL HIS SKILLS! DURING HIS 13-POINT STREAK, HE HIT A TURNAROUND J, A LAY-UP, A DUNK, A HOOK SHOT AND SOME FOUL SHOTS, AND HE GRABBED 5 BOARDS! AMAZING!

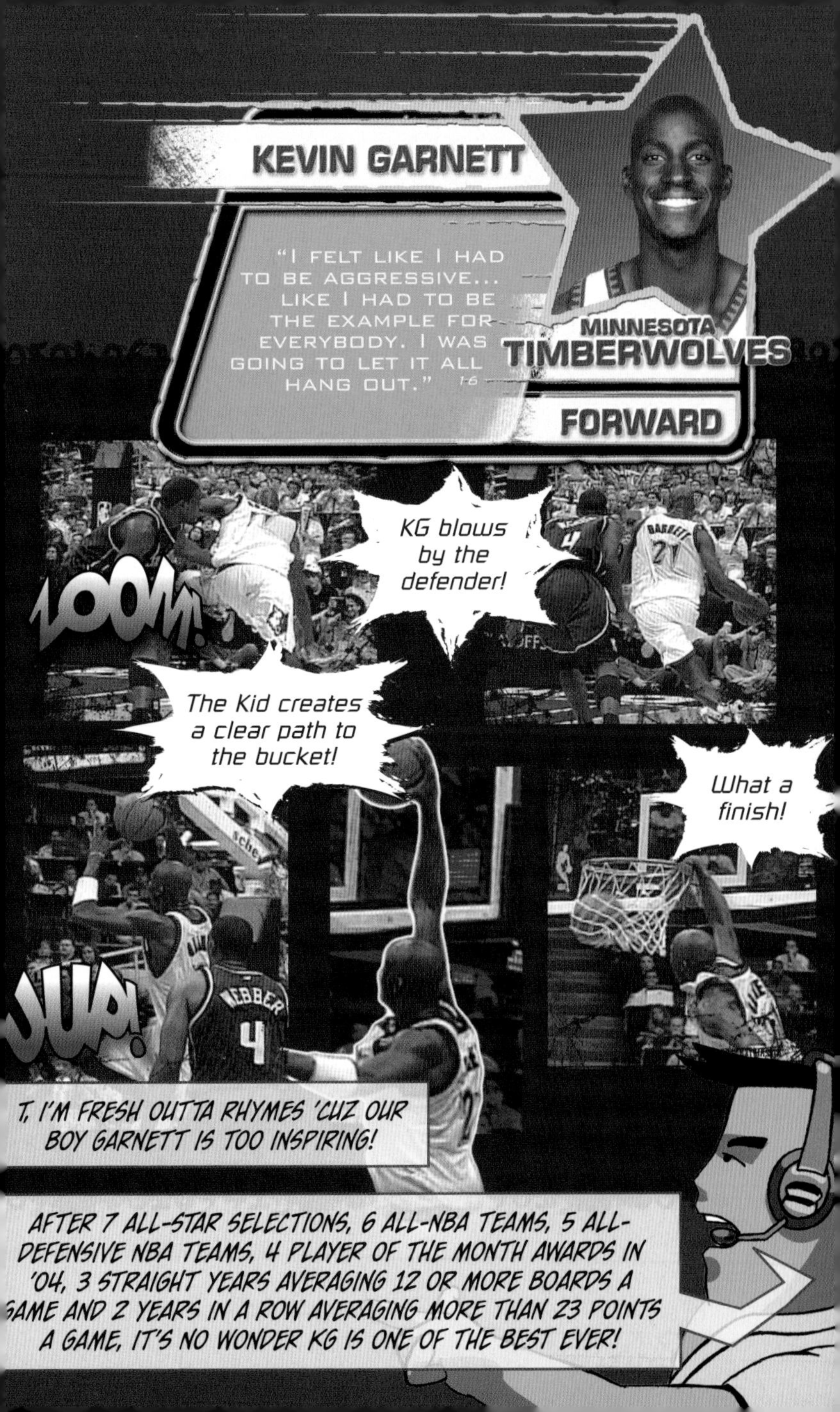
KEVIN GARNETT
"I FELT LIKE I HAD TO BE AGGRESSIVE... LIKE I HAD TO BE THE EXAMPLE FOR EVERYBODY. I WAS GOING TO LET IT ALL HANG OUT." [1-6]
MINNESOTA TIMBERWOLVES
FORWARD
ZOOM!
KG blows by the defender!
The Kid creates a clear path to the bucket!
What a finish!
T, I'M FRESH OUTTA RHYMES 'CUZ OUR BOY GARNETT IS TOO INSPIRING!
AFTER 7 ALL-STAR SELECTIONS, 6 ALL-NBA TEAMS, 5 ALL-DEFENSIVE NBA TEAMS, 4 PLAYER OF THE MONTH AWARDS IN '04, 3 STRAIGHT YEARS AVERAGING 12 OR MORE BOARDS A GAME AND 2 YEARS IN A ROW AVERAGING MORE THAN 23 POINTS A GAME, IT'S NO WONDER KG IS ONE OF THE BEST EVER!

May 29, 2004: KG Keeps Wolves Alive in Game 5!

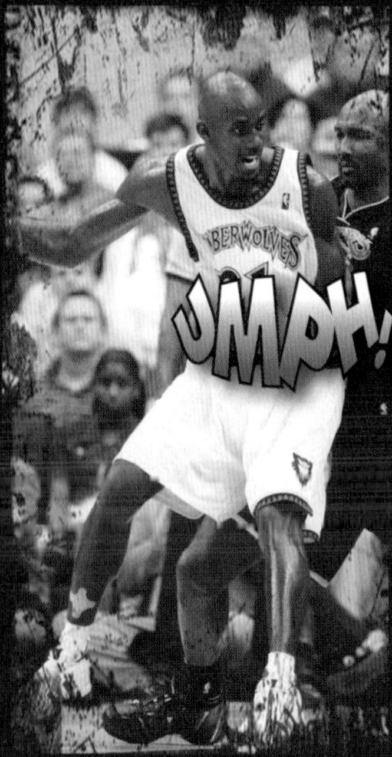
UMPH!

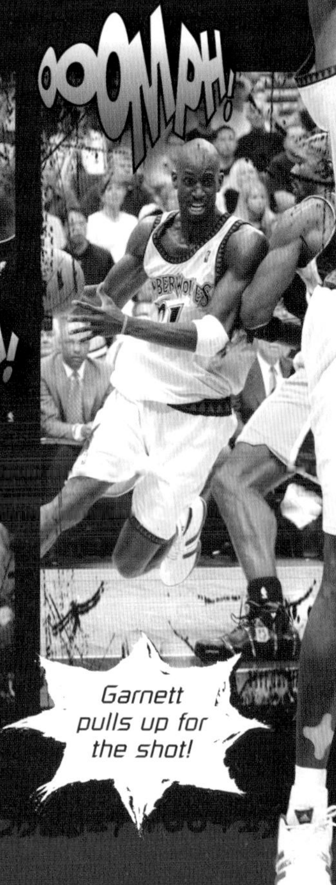
OOOMPH!
Garnett pulls up for the shot!

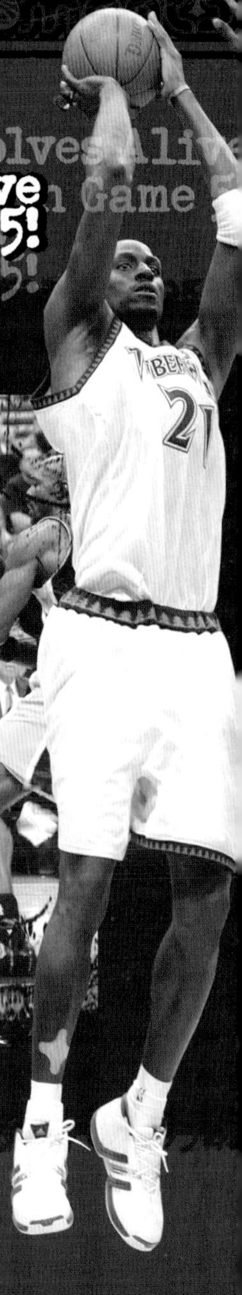

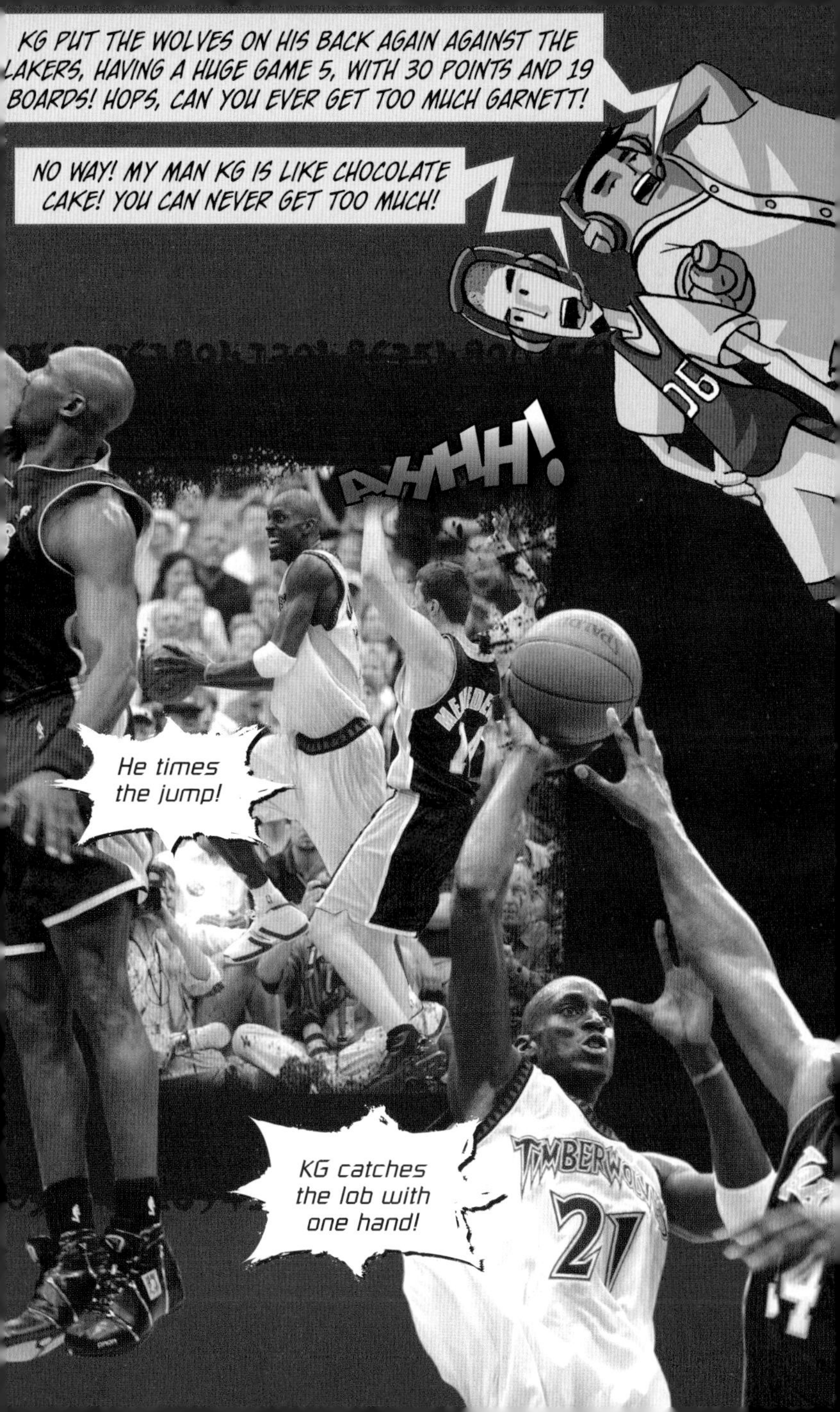
KG PUT THE WOLVES ON HIS BACK AGAIN AGAINST THE LAKERS, HAVING A HUGE GAME 5, WITH 30 POINTS AND 19 BOARDS! HOPS, CAN YOU EVER GET TOO MUCH GARNETT!
NO WAY! MY MAN KG IS LIKE CHOCOLATE CAKE! YOU CAN NEVER GET TOO MUCH!
AHHH!
He times the jump!
KG catches the lob with one hand!
TIMBERWOLVES
21

for the books

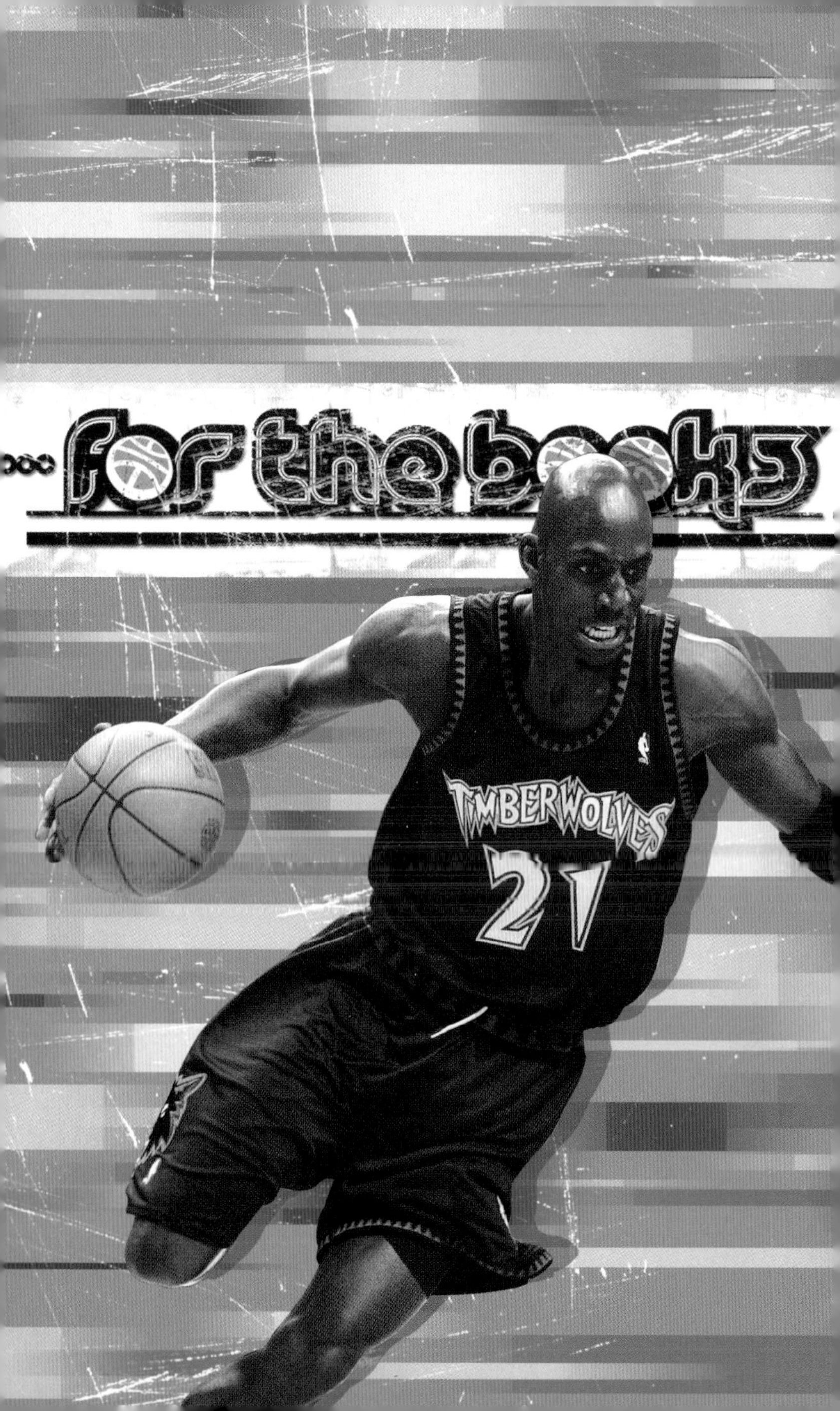
TIMBERWOLVES
21

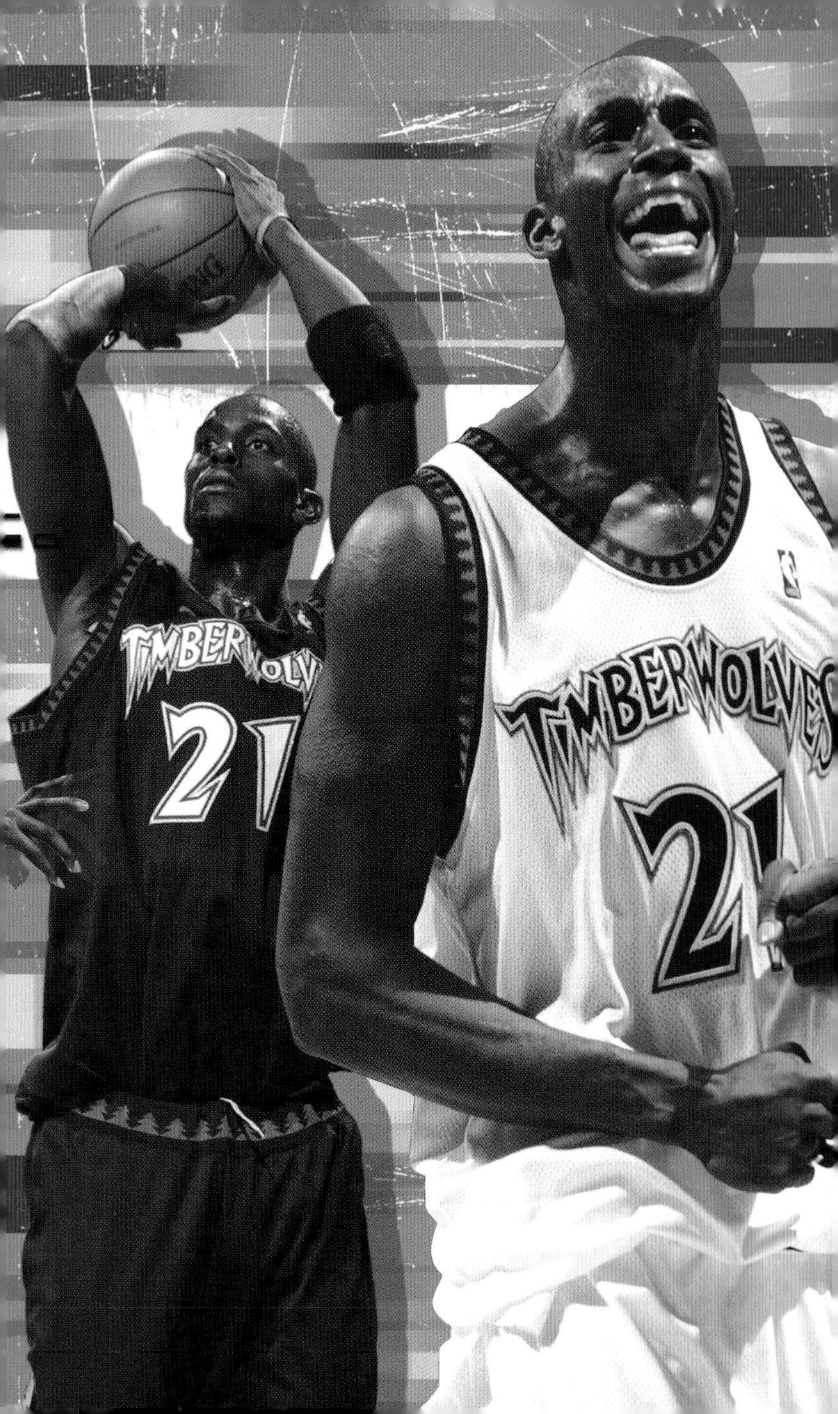
TIMBERWOLVES
21
TIMBERWOLVES
21

TIMELINE

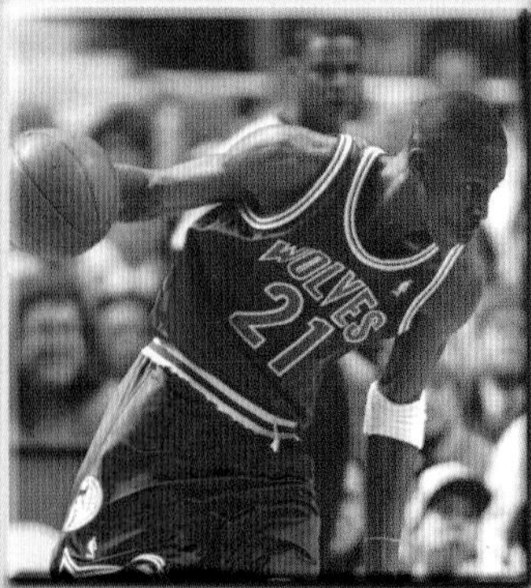
WOLVES
21

1995 Garnett is selected as the number five overall pick in the 1995 NBA draft, the first player to make the leap from high school to the NBA in 20 years!

1996 Named to the NBA All-Rookie Second Team.

1997 Selected to his first NBA All-Star Game.

1998 Started his first NBA All-Star Game. One of only four players in the NBA to record 100 steals and 100 blocks.

2000 Became only the ninth player in history to average 20-10-5 for the season.

Named NBA Player of the Week THREE times.

Named NBA Player of the MONTH for January.

Named to All-NBA Third Team.

2001 Named to the Second Team All-NBA.

Named to the All-Defensive First Team.

Finished second to Dikembe Mutombo for Defensive Player of the Year.

Became the T-Wolves all-time leading scorer.

2002 Had third straight season of averaging 20 PPG, 10 RPG, 5 APG (fifth player ever to do it).

Finished second in the League with 59 double-doubles.

Named to the All-Interview First Team.

2003	Posted team single-season records in rebounds (1,102) and minutes (3,321).

Named to the First Team All-NBA.

Selected to the First-Team NBA All-Defensive Team.

Finished second in MVP voting.

Finished ninth in the NBA in scoring and 2nd in rebounding.

2004	Won the League MVP Award.

Won his first playoff series against the Nuggets.

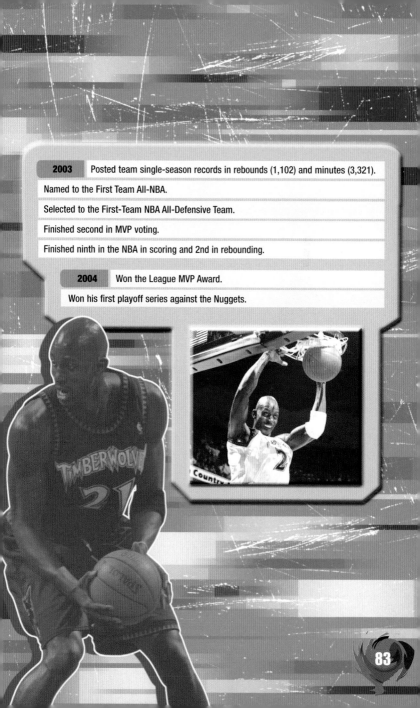

GARNETT INDEX: COOL STATS AND FACTS!

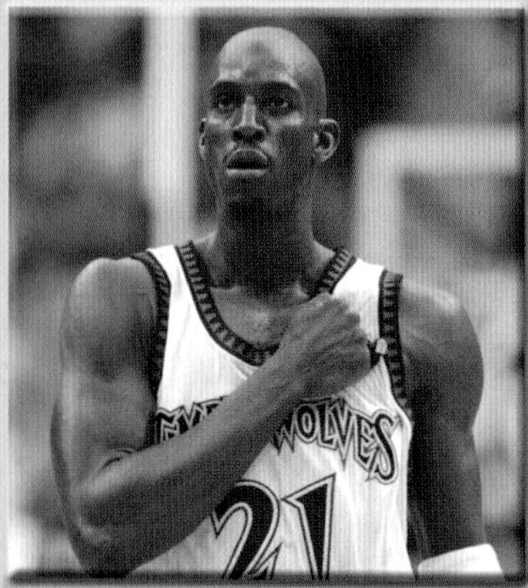
WOLVES
21

Title of Garnett's first *Sports Illustrated* Cover: "Ready or not..."

The two athletes Garnett lists as his heroes: Magic Johnson and Tony Dorsett.

KG's age at the end of his NBA rookie season: 19 years, 11 months.

Number of games KG started his rookie year: 43.

The name of Garnett's clothing line: OBF (Official Block Family).

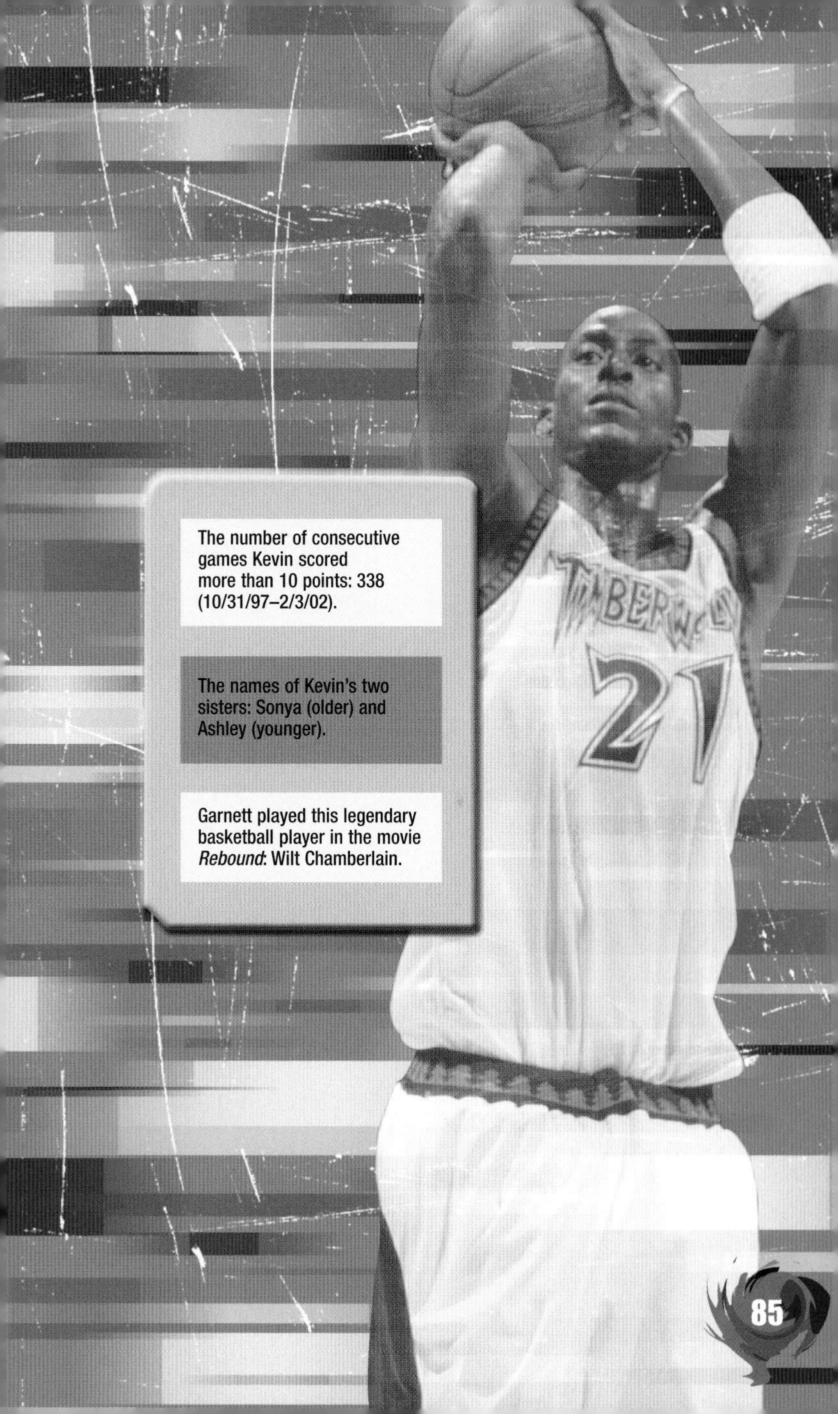
21

The number of consecutive games Kevin scored more than 10 points: 338 (10/31/97–2/3/02).

The names of Kevin's two sisters: Sonya (older) and Ashley (younger).

Garnett played this legendary basketball player in the movie *Rebound*: Wilt Chamberlain.

GARNETT INDEX:
COOL STATS AND FACTS!

The most NBA games KG has played in a row: 181 from 12/11/96 to 4/14/99.

Number of seasons in a row Garnett averaged 20 points, 10 rebounds, 5 assists: 5.

The only other player in NBA history to do that: Larry Bird.

The three foods KG lists as his favorites: hamburgers, french fries and pizza.

The number of categories KG ranked in the top 10 in the NBA in 2004: 20.

KG's favorite basketball team growing up: Los Angeles Lakers.

KG became the first ever NBA player to do this in the 2004 season: Win three consecutive Player of the Month honors (December, January, February).

With Garnett's 3,000th career assist, he became the 17th player in NBA history to achieve this feat: 13,000 points, 7,000 boards, 3,000 assists!

MILESTONES

REGULAR SEASON HIGHS

POINTS: 40 two times
REBOUNDS: 25 vs. Sacramento 12/5/03
ASSISTS: 12 two times
STEALS: 7 vs. Atlanta 12/14/99
BLOCKS: 8 two times

PLAYOFF HIGHS

POINTS: 35 vs. Lakers 4/22/03
REBOUNDS: 22 vs. Denver 4/21/04
ASSISTS: 10 vs. Denver 4/21/04
STEALS: 4 vs. Sacramento 5/19/04
BLOCKS: 6 vs. Sacramento 5/8/04

Photo credits//:

All photos courtesy of NBA Entertainment/Getty Images. All additional images from video footage courtesy of NBA Entertainment.

Cover: Jed Jacobsohn
Page 3: Elsa
Page 4: Clockwise from top left: David Sherman; Barry Gossage; Jesse D. Garrabrant; David Sherman
Page 5: Jed Jacobsohn
Page 7: Bob Binder
Page 8: Stephen Dunn
Page 9: From top: David Taylor; Brian Bahr; Harry How
Page 10: From left: David Sherman; Rocky Widner
Page 11: Top left: Craig Lassig. Bottom left: Fernando Medina. Large photo: Brian Babineau
Page 12: Large photo and photo at right: Brian Bahr
Page 13: From left: Brian Bahr; Elsa
Page 14: From left: Todd Warshaw; Sam Forencich
Page 15: Top photo: Joe Murphy. Below, from left: Todd Warshaw; Otto Greule
Page 16: From left: Sam Forencich; Andy Hayt
Page 17: From left: Otto Greule; Rocky Widner
Page 18: Top row, from left: Jesse Garrabrant; Jesse Garrabrant; Jed Jacobsohn. Middle row, from left: Jed Jacobsohn; Elsa; Elsa. Bottom row, from left: David Sherman; David Sherman; Jesse Garrabrant
Page 19: Noah Graham
Page 20: Barry Gossage
Page 22: Large photo: Rocky Widner. Bottom photo: Nathaniel S. Butler
Page 24: Large photo: David Sherman. Bottom photo: Scott Cunningham
Page 26: Barry Gossage
Page 28: Noren Trotman
Page 30: Large photo: Jed Jacobsohn. Bottom photo: David Sherman
Page 32: Rocky Widner
Page 34: Elsa
Page 36: Large photo: Rocky Widner. Bottom photo: David Sherman
Page 38: From left: Jesse D. Garrabrant; Elsa
Page 39: From left: Noah Graham; Jed Jacobsohn
Page 40: Jed Jacobsohn
Page 41: David Sherman
Page 43: Large photo: Garrett Ellwood. Bottom photo: David Sherman
Page 44: David Sherman
Page 47: Bottom photo: Rocky Widner
Page 48: David Sherman
Page 49: Fernando Medina
Page 51: Large photo: David Sherman
Page 53: Large photo: Noah Graham. Bottom photo: Barry Gossage
Page 55: Large photo: Rocky Widner
Page 56: Left photo: Jed Jacobsohn. Middle photo: Rocky Widner. Right photo: Rocky Widner
Page 57: Top photo: Rocky Widner. Bottom photos from left: Rocky Widner; Jed Jacobsohn
Page 59: Barry Gossage
Page 61: Sam Forencich
Page 62: Photo at left: David Sherman. Large photo at right of Garnett: Rocky Widner.
Page 63: From left: Andrew D. Bernstein; David Sherma
Page 64: From left: Andrew D. Bernstein; Jesse D. Garrabrant
Page 65: Top photo: Gary Bassing. Bottom photos from left: Jesse D. Garrabrant; David Sherman
Page 66: From left: Catherine Steenkeste; Jed Jacobsohn; Jed Jacobsohn
Page 67: Both photos: Elsa
Page 69: Top photo: Michael Lebrecht. Large photo: Elsa
Page 70: Jed Jacobson
Page 71: Top photo: Glenn James
Page 72: Andrew D. Bernstein
Page 75: Top photo: Steve Yeater
Page 76: Large photo: David Sherman
Page 77: Top photo: David Sherman
Page 78: All photos: Jed Jacobsohn
Page 79: Photo at left: Jed Jacobsohn. Middle photo: Elsa. Photo at bottom right: Jed Jacobsohn
Page 80: Jed Jacobsohn
Page 81: From left: Garrett Ellwood; David Sherman
Page 82: Brian Bahr
Page 83: From left: Jed Jacobsohn; David Sherman
Page 84: From left: Elsa; Barry Gossage
Page 85: David Sherman
Page 86: From left: Jesse D. Garrabrant; Sam Forencich
Page 87: Top: David Sherman. Bottom: Brian Babineau

SOURCES//:

1 KEVIN MCHALE FROM THE T-WOLVES WEBSITE, ARTICLE BY RACHEL BACHMAN NOVEMBER 22, 1995

2 HUBIE BROWN FROM MINNEAPOLIS STAR TRIBUNE, ARTICLE BY STEVE ASCHBURNER FEBRUARY 15, 2004

3 PAUL SILAS FROM MINNEAPOLIS STAR TRIBUNE, ARTICLE BY STEVE ASCHBURNER FEBRUARY 15, 2004

4 SHAREEF ABDUR-RAHIM FROM MINNEAPOLIS STAR TRIBUNE, ARTICLE BY STEVE ASCHBURNER FEBRUARY 15, 2004

FLIP SAUNDERS FROM MINNEAPOLIS STAR TRIBUNE, ARTICLE BY STEVE ASCHBURNER FEBRUARY 15, 2004

KEVIN GARNETT FROM MINNEAPOLIS STAR TRIBUNE, ARTICLE BY STEVE ASCHBURNER FEBRUARY 15, 2004

KEVIN GARNETT FROM MINNEAPOLIS STAR TRIBUNE, ARTICLE BY STEVE ASCHBURNER JANUARY 30, 2004

8 MARK MADSEN FROM MINNEAPOLIS STAR TRIBUNE, ARTICLE BY STEVE ASCHBURNER FEBRUARY 15, 2004

TRACY MCGRADY FROM MINNEAPOLIS STAR TRIBUNE, ARTICLE BY STEVE ASCHBURNER FEBRUARY 15, 2004

10 TOM GUGLIOTTA FROM NBA.COM POST GAME QUOTES ON APRIL 17, 2004

11 RICK ADELMAN FROM NBA.COM POST GAME QUOTES ON MAY 19, 2004

12 DON NELSON FROM SPORTS ILLUSTRATED.COM, ARTICLE BY IAN THOMPSON JULY 2, 2004

TRACY MCGRADY FROM MINNEAPOLIS STAR TRIBUNE, ARTICLE BY STEVE ASCHBURNER FEBRUARY 15, 2004

14 LATRELL SPREWELL FROM NBA.COM POST GAME QUOTES ON MAY 19, 2004

15 CHRIS WEBBER FROM NBA.COM POST GAME QUOTES ON MAY 19, 2004

16 KEVIN GARNETT FROM NBA.COM (SPORTSTICKER ARTICLE) MAY 19, 2004

TOKYOPOP THANKS//:
JOHN HAREAS AND
MICHAEL LEVINE
OF THE NBA

ALSO AVAILABLE FROM TOKYOPOP®

MANGA

.HACK//LEGEND OF THE TWILIGHT
ALICHINO
ANGELIC LAYER
BABY BIRTH
BRAIN POWERED
BRIGADOON
B'TX
CANDIDATE FOR GODDESS, THE
CARDCAPTOR SAKURA
CARDCAPTOR SAKURA - MASTER OF THE CLOW
CHRONICLES OF THE CURSED SWORD
CLAMP SCHOOL DETECTIVES
CLOVER
COMIC PARTY
CORRECTOR YUI
COWBOY BEBOP
COWBOY BEBOP: SHOOTING STAR
CRESCENT MOON
CROSS
CULDCEPT
CYBORG 009
D•N•ANGEL
DEARS
DEMON DIARY
DEMON ORORON, THE
DIGIMON
DIGIMON TAMERS
DIGIMON ZERO TWO
DRAGON HUNTER
DRAGON KNIGHTS
DRAGON VOICE
DREAM SAGA
DUKLYON: CLAMP SCHOOL DEFENDERS
ET CETERA
ETERNITY
FAERIES' LANDING
FLCL
FLOWER OF THE DEEP SLEEP
FORBIDDEN DANCE
FRUITS BASKET
G GUNDAM
GATEKEEPERS
GIRL GOT GAME
GUNDAM SEED ASTRAY
GUNDAM WING
GUNDAM WING: BATTLEFIELD OF PACIFISTS
GUNDAM WING: ENDLESS WALTZ
GUNDAM WING: THE LAST OUTPOST (G-UNIT)
HANDS OFF!

HARLEM BEAT
HYPER RUNE
I.N.V.U.
INITIAL D
INSTANT TEEN: JUST ADD NUTS
JING: KING OF BANDITS
JING: KING OF BANDITS - TWILIGHT TALES
JULINE
KARE KANO
KILL ME, KISS ME
KINDAICHI CASE FILES, THE
KING OF HELL
KODOCHA: SANA'S STAGE
LEGEND OF CHUN HYANG, THE
LOVE OR MONEY
MAGIC KNIGHT RAYEARTH I
MAGIC KNIGHT RAYEARTH II
MAN OF MANY FACES
MARMALADE BOY
MARS
MARS: HORSE WITH NO NAME
MINK
MIRACLE GIRLS
MODEL
MOURYOU KIDEN: LEGEND OF THE NYMPH
NECK AND NECK
ONE
ONE I LOVE, THE
PEACH FUZZ
PEACH GIRL
PEACH GIRL: CHANGE OF HEART
PITA-TEN
PLANET LADDER
PLANETES
PRESIDENT DAD
PRINCESS AI
PSYCHIC ACADEMY
QUEEN'S KNIGHT, THE
RAGNAROK
RAVE MASTER
REALITY CHECK
REBIRTH
REBOUND
RISING STARS OF MANGA
SAILOR MOON
SAINT TAIL
SAMURAI GIRL REAL BOUT HIGH SCHOOL
SEIKAI TRILOGY, THE
SGT. FROG
SHAOLIN SISTERS

09.21

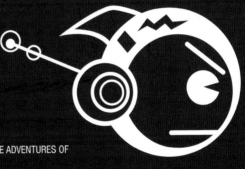

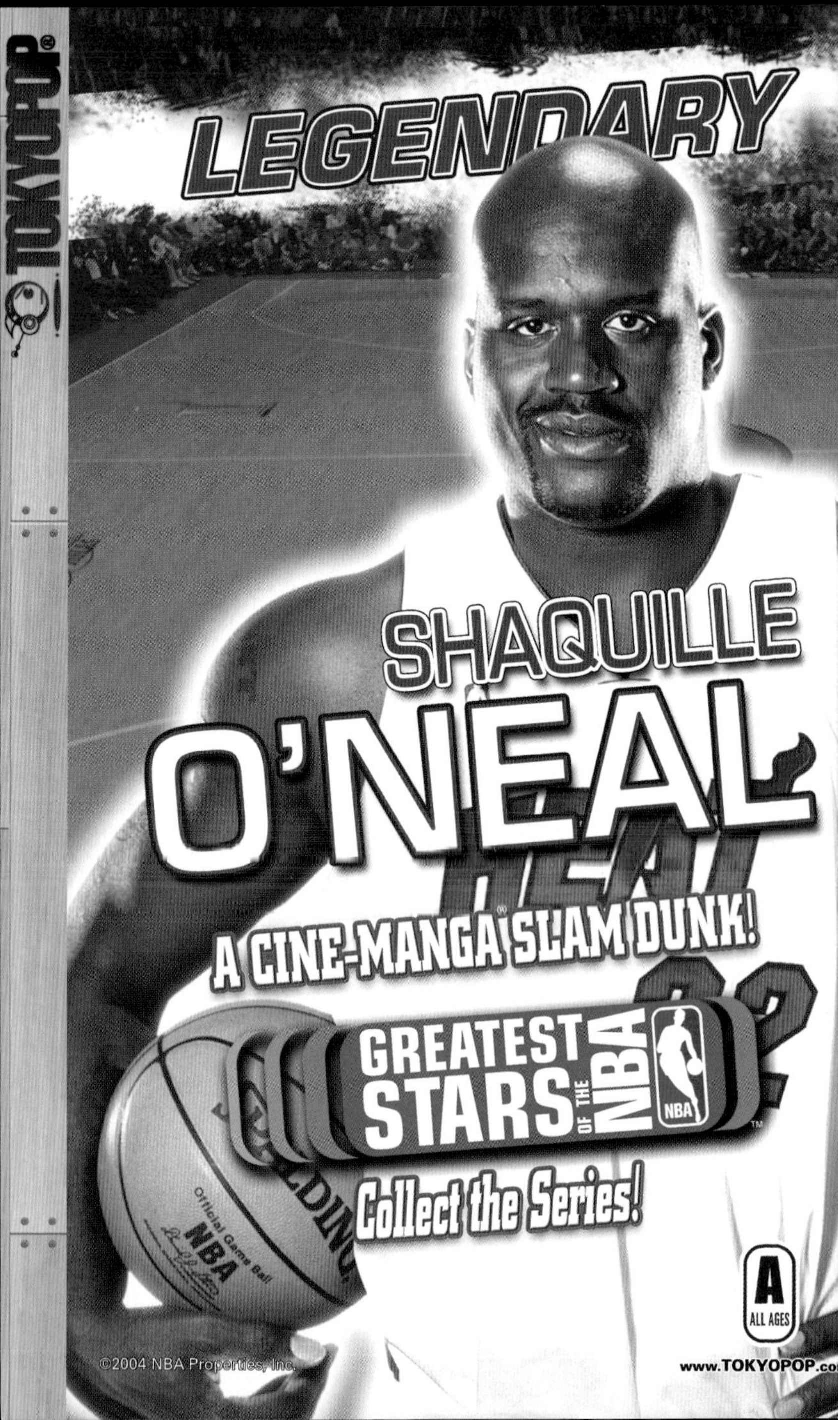

TOKYOPOP
LEGENDARY
SHAQUILLE
O'NEAL
A CINE-MANGA SLAM DUNK!
GREATEST STARS OF THE NBA
Collect the Series!
A
ALL AGES
©2004 NBA Properties, Inc.
www.TOKYOPOP.com

DOMINATING

TIM
DUNCAN

A CINE-MANGA SLAM DUNK!

GREATEST
STARS OF THE NBA

Collect the Series!

TOKYOPOP

A
ALL AGES

www.TOKYOPOP.com

UNSTOPPABLE

JASON KIDD

A CINE-MANGA SLAM DUNK!

GREATEST STARS OF THE **NBA**

Collect the Series!

A — ALL AGES